Albert Speer –
Escaping the Gallows

Albert Speer – Escaping the Gallows

Secret Conversations with Hitler's Top Nazi

Adrian Greaves

Pen & Sword
MILITARY

First published in Great Britain in 2021 by
Pen & Sword Military
An imprint of
Pen & Sword Books Ltd
Yorkshire – Philadelphia

ISBN 978 1 39900 953 9

Typeset by Mac Style
Printed and bound by CPI Group (UK) Ltd, Croydon, CR0 4YY

Pen & Sword Books Limited incorporates the imprints of Atlas,
Archaeology, Aviation, Discovery, Family History, Fiction, History,
Maritime, Military, Military Classics, Politics, Select, Transport,
True Crime, Air World, Frontline Publishing, Leo Cooper, Remember
When, Seaforth Publishing, The Praetorian Press, Wharncliffe
Local History, Wharncliffe Transport, Wharncliffe True Crime
and White Owl.

For a complete list of Pen & Sword titles please contact

PEN & SWORD BOOKS LIMITED
47 Church Street, Barnsley, South Yorkshire, S70 2AS, England
E-mail: enquiries@pen-and-sword.co.uk
Website: www.pen-and-sword.co.uk

Or

PEN AND SWORD BOOKS
1950 Lawrence Rd, Havertown, PA 19083, USA
E-mail: Uspen-and-sword@casematepublishers.com
Website: www.penandswordbooks.com

Contents

Introduction

Meeting Albert Speer

'More beguiling and dangerous than Hitler who had died before in the ruins of Berlin.'[1]

On the night of 10 May 1941, Hitler's deputy, Rudolf Hess, made a remarkable solo flight from Augsburg in southern Germany to Scotland in a misguided personal attempt to seek peace between Germany and Britain. At the time, the German High Command was under serious pressure from having to fight on two fronts, the British in the west, the Russians to the east. Hess's logic was to arrange peace with Britain to enable German forces to be concentrated on the Russian Eastern Front. His flight was undertaken in complete secrecy and without the knowledge or authority of Hitler. In total darkness he parachuted from his plane leaving it to crash near Glasgow and on landing in a field he was immediately detained by local farmers pending the arrival of police. Within hours his true identity was revealed whereupon Churchill ordered that he was not to be pandered to, but to be deliberately treated as a prisoner of war. He was initially taken to the Tower of London then, for the duration of the war, he was held prisoner in Wales. Hitler declared Hess 'insane'.

A year later, my recently married father-to-be, an officer in the Royal Artillery Regiment, was on a course in Wales before being posted to India; my mother worked as a typist in one of the government ministries in London. One weekend my father was unexpectedly detailed to command an escort that took Hess to Surrey, believed by my father for medical reasons. That weekend, my parents somehow managed to meet in London, and nine months later I was born in the middle of an air raid, I suppose, courtesy of Rudolf Hess.

Eighteen years later (1961), I was commissioned into the army and posted to the Welch Regiment then serving in West Berlin, a divided city more than 100 miles behind the then 'Iron Curtain' dividing the Allied West

Germany and the Soviet occupied East Germany. My arrival there coincided with the construction of the Berlin Wall and a seriously worsening Cold War situation. During the two exciting years that followed, I was regularly detailed as the duty guard commander at Spandau Prison which housed the three most senior surviving Second World War Nazi war criminals, Rudolf Hess, Baldur von Schirach and Albert Speer. All three had narrowly escaped execution on the gallows following their trials at the 1946 International Military Tribunal at Nuremberg and were part-way through long prison sentences. While performing this duty for the first time, a regular task for junior officers, and knowing of my father's brief time escorting him, I hoped for a sight of Rudolf Hess. Instead I unexpectedly found myself standing next to Hess outside his cell in the prison corridor. As his flight to Scotland had brought about my very existence, and in very shaky German, I thanked him; he ignored me and walked away.

However, Albert Speer overheard my words and quietly asked for an explanation. Unsure of prison protocol I stepped back but the governor accompanying me indicated I could speak to Speer who then invited me to join him in the prison garden. Naturally I accepted, after all, Speer had been Hitler's longtime friend and Reich armaments minister. We had a friendly chat, the first of many such discreet but unofficial meetings. Thereafter I was regularly able to meet with him, and, with his full co-operation, and even enthusiasm, over the next two years we amicably discussed an array of subjects, including the delicate question of his and German guilt for war crimes. At his trial Speer had successfully protested his personal innocence of, or participation in, war crimes against humanity, but accepted vicarious responsibility having been a senior minister of Hitler, for which he was sentenced to twenty years imprisonment in Spandau. Our highly unofficial discussions were a remarkable opportunity for a young army officer to acquire a singular and in-depth insight into this influential man's memories of Hitler and of his thoughts during his fifteen years as a Nazi minister. Our conversations were especially unique because Speer was still serving his sentence and, apart from his co-defendants, Schirach and the delusional Hess, he was completely isolated from the outside world or any press media. Despite our disparate ages and rank differences, he clearly enjoyed our many conversations, which I noted at the time, and his attitude to me was always friendly and courteous, and he spoke excellent English. Conversely, neither Hess nor Schirach would ever speak with me.

Following his much publicized release from Spandau in 1966, I watched Speer manipulate the enthusiastic media to perpetuate and develop his original 'not me' defence which had saved him from the Nuremberg gallows. This line of defence, and by sticking to his story, was necessary for him to re-establish himself among post-war Germans. By the time of his release, his fellow countrymen were steadily progressing towards international acceptance, from being a nation of shattered war-weary people to being desperately in need of a 'good German' to help repair the terrible reputation of their deeply shamed country. Speer soon succeeded beyond all expectations and almost became an elder statesman, much respected in Germany and internationally, and sought out by the media and politicians who all treated him with reverence. But was Speer as innocent as he portrayed himself, or was he the master of the ultimate confidence trick?

Albert Speer: Hitler's top Nazi, friend and Armaments Minister
Name: Albert Speer.
Born: 19 March 1905, Mannheim, Germany.
Died: 1 September 1981, London.

As the years accelerate us away from the terrible memories of German atrocities in the Second World War, itself a much written-about subject, one complex question remains unanswered, and it continues to haunt the German people, notwithstanding the healing passage of time. The question was the focus of my conversations with Speer and was in two parts; what did the German people know about the savagery being conducted in their name across Europe until Germany's defeat – and secondly, did they care? The question is complex and remains sufficiently open to continue to cause modern day Germans considerable national *angst* and personal 'guilt by association' for their country's predilection for brutality in times of war. Even contemporary historians have struggled to understand and explain this civilised and sophisticated nation's policy of organised and systematic wartime brutality, a prominent German phenomenon since Germanic tribes once waged war across central Europe and then dominated their victims. They saw themselves as the *Herrenvolk*, the 'master race', and naturally superior to other races. This ingrained national superiority then gave rise to the German belief that they were, somehow, the paramount Aryan race set apart from other non-German ethnic groups, and by the end of the nineteenth-century, they viewed themselves as both the superior and dominant power in Europe. Interracial mixing was frowned upon and there were legal policies in both Germany and its African colonies which banned mixed marriages on racial and moral grounds.

With German industry and ship building developing new markets and with naval prestige steadily strengthening, Germany sought to further increase its status as both a European and world power. In Germany's fledgling colonies, official colonial social policy was directed at social differentiation and segregation in order to maintain their perceived racial purity and German superiority. By then, German cultural ideology founded on the innate German urge for domination was firmly anchored to the basic principle that subject natives must be made to work for their new overlords, and without any rights; concomitantly, German colonial military law required harsh measures when deemed necessary to maintain or enforce order.

As Africa entered the twentieth-century, the German agenda was set for the most unpleasant action, action that paved the way for the worst excesses of atrocities against those hapless tribes who found themselves under German military occupation. For example, the first years of the early 1900s witnessed the European 'scramble for Africa' during which German troops officially and systematically used brutality and mass murder of local populations as an acceptable means of gaining and maintaining control across their new dominions. Records reveal some 80,000 resisting *Herero* and *Namaqua* people in German South West Africa (Namibia) and over 250,000 people in German East Africa (Tanzania) were killed by over-work and exhaustion, starvation or mass murder.

Then, at the beginning of the First World War and commencing in neutral Belgium, the invading German army sent to attack France engaged in numerous atrocities against overrun civilian populations; this behaviour was viewed with disdain by the world's press but a few years earlier it might have been seen as 'understandable' when suppressing resisting Africans. But for a modern European power invading its equally modern neighbours, such action was shocking and unexpected, and seemingly out of character. In any event, such behaviour was in complete violation of the treaties of the fifth convention of the Hague Conference, countersigned by Germany. For example, for five days in 1914, beginning 25 August, the city of Louvain was subjected to mass destruction by German troops who plundered the town before setting it on fire and executing hundreds of protesting civilians. This atrocity was followed by the massacre in the village of Dinant, near Liege, in which German soldiers killed some 700 civilians on the orders of their corps commander. Similarly, on the way into France, German forces looted and destroyed villages, and much of the countryside in their path, indiscriminately killing significant numbers of civilians, including women and children.

Later, in 1936, and with Germany prospering and relentlessly rearming its military, Hitler took the opportunity of giving his Luftwaffe pilots live battle experience by sending some 16,000 German troops to assist the nationalist General Franco in Spain's civil war. On 31 March, German military aircraft attacked and bombed the unprotected and unsuspecting towns of Vizcaya and Durango, where 250 civilians died including the priest, nuns and congregation attending a church ceremony. On 26 April, German dive bombers attacked the town of Guernica; it was one of the most controversial events of the Spanish Civil War, with 1,654 dead and 889 wounded civilians. News of the severity of these air raids was greeted in Germany with pride and elation, but the action shocked and alarmed politicians and military leaders across Europe and America. Then, at dawn on 31 May 1937, the German pocket battleship, *Admiral Scheer*, supported by four German destroyers, attacked the Spanish port of Almeria. Then, without warning, the German ships fired hundreds of shells into the adjacent city, killing 20 civilians as the residents fled in panic, wounding 50 more and destroying 35 buildings. German ruthlessness towards civilian populations was blatant; world leaders were in no doubt that Germany's involvement in Spain was an excuse for a full public rehearsal for any future German campaign.

By the time Hitler rose to power, the German people were familiar with the concept of linking military aggression with ruthless oppression and overt brutality to instil terror among subjugated civilian populations. The Nazis were uncompromising about their perceived low status of their non-German victims, specially Jews and East Europeans, who were classified by the Nazis as *Untermenschen* or sub-humans; as such they were to be excluded from the system of moral rights and obligations that bonds humankind to the extent that it was wrong to kill a person, but permissible to exterminate 'non humans'.[2] This pre-existing racially-based and murderous inclination somehow justified the Germans' brutal treatment of specified groups, starting with their own disabled, the mentally retarded and then the Jews, all were treated as though they were sub-human creatures. The German people could not have been left in any doubt as to Hitler's intentions for the Jews; he had openly declared his intentions in his widely published *Mein Kampf*, first published in Germany in 1932 when he wrote:

If you ask me what I mean by depopulation, I will tell you that I mean the removal of entire racial units, and that is what I intend to accomplish; this, bluntly speaking, is my objective. I have the right to remove millions of the lower races.

The policy of legal murder soon extended to eliminate all dissenters of Nazism, and then, as the war progressed, it was extended to include certain categories of prisoners of war, especially those from Russia and Eastern Europe.

But this book focuses not on the Germans as a people but on one highly intelligent German, Professor Albert Speer, who was at the pinnacle of Nazi Party leadership from the beginning of Hitler's rise to power in the 1930s through to the end of the war in 1945. From his earliest association with Hitler, Speer understood Hitler's intention to eliminate the Jews. From 1938 onwards, Speer personally oversaw the state's anti-Semitic policy which commenced when he ordered the ruthless eviction of Berlin's Jews from their homes, often without warning, as part of Speer's (unfulfilled) plan for the construction of Hitler's new German capital, *Germania*. Speer later claimed he was unaware that Jews evicted by his various departments from their homes and businesses were force marched to railway yards to be packed into wagons destined for various extermination camps, usually in Poland, or to work as forced labour in Speer's factories.

By the end of the war, Speer had become Hitler's second-in-command and, by implication, complicit with Hitler's plan and methods for total world domination. Yet, post-war, having narrowly escaped the Allied' war crimes gallows at Nuremberg, he became famous as the Nazi leader who 'knew nothing', mainly on the basis that the mass murder of Jews and prisoners of war had taken place beyond Germany's borders; this enabled Albert Speer, and a number of other senior Germans, to deny knowledge thereof. By having been a wartime compliant accomplice to Hitler's orders, and then after Germany's defeat by claiming innocence of crimes against humanity, this one man exemplifies the whole question of German guilty knowledge.

Before and during the Second World War, Albert Speer was Hitler's confidant, almost his only friend, as well as being the Nazi minister responsible for armaments production. After Hitler's death in 1945, Speer was arrested by the British for war crimes. He was then prosecuted by the victorious Allies at the 1946 Nuremberg International War Crimes Tribunal where he beguiled the Allied judges with his version of events and heartfelt pretentions of innocence, thereby saving his life. Most of his fellow senior

Nazis were convicted of war crimes; they were sentenced to death and, within days, executed in a most barbaric manner by an incompetent and untrained American executioner. Of all those arraigned before the court, only Speer and seven of his co-defendants were spared the gallows but, nevertheless, in the depth of a night, they had to listen to their former colleagues under sentence of death being forcibly taken from their cells to the gallows in the lower wing of the building.[3] The following morning, Speer and his seven fellow prisoners were obliged to wash down and clean the execution room.

Although the Russian judges demanded Speer be executed, he was instead sentenced by a majority of the Allied judges to twenty years imprisonment, which he served from 1946 to 1966 in Berlin's bleak Spandau Prison. Having been found 'not guilty' at Nuremberg of the worst Nazi crimes against humanity, Speer became internationally known as the 'good German' for admitting being a Nazi minister and, by association, guilty of Nazi crimes – but not of crimes against humanity. After his release from prison in 1966, he set about manipulating the media with his strategy of professed innocence and thereby became a respected role model for post-war Germans, still desperate for some evidence that, somehow, ordinary people were oblivious to the countless atrocities, conducted on an industrial scale, committed in their name. With such a highly placed, highly respected, and popular figure apparently unaware of his Nazi government's orders for atrocities and exterminations across Europe, he succeeded in strengthening the collective subconscious of post-war Germans that they too, could also be equally innocent.

In Britain today, Albert Speer is all but forgotten. As the result of his demeanour, contriteness, and admissions of 'third party' guilt at the Nuremberg trials, he is still remembered in Germany as being the 'good German' of the Second World War, as opposed to being remembered for his role as the overseer of mass Jewish evictions in Berlin, as the constructor of concentration camps and prodigious facilitator of slave labour from vanquished nations.[4] Also overlooked was his wartime achievement as the minister who deliberately prolonged the war by several months, which resulted in the further loss of millions of lives; in January 1945 nearly half a million German soldiers were killed – more than Britain and America lost in the whole war, with a further quarter million in each of the following three months until the war's end.

Following his release from Spandau in 1966, he undertook numerous interviews with the media, and his flurry of best-selling books rapidly made him popular and highly respected. This veneration grew inestimably even after his untimely death aged 76 in a London hotel room where he was resting with his young mistress following a BBC interview. After his death, all the enigmas and 'good German' accounts that had surrounded him following his release from prison came under scrutiny; previously unseen documents, letters and photographs containing damning evidence of his deeds began to surface.

At the same time, a steady stream of accounts from psychologists, military historians and academics began to be published; all keen to use their professional skills to explain the inexplicable; how a 28-year-old and out-of-work architect could be invited to become such an important adviser and friend to Hitler, and then become the Führer's senior Reich Minister without apparently knowing what the Nazi Party was doing. Towards the end of the war, Speer became the second most powerful man in Germany to the frail and drug impaired delusional Hitler. Then, having escaped the Nuremberg hangman and completed his twenty-year prison sentence for war crimes, he was handsomely paid by the world's press and media, desperate to understand and report how he could have so innocently but willingly served such a vile regime. During the war years, he controlled Germany's war production, while maintaining that his country's savage treatment of the Jews and concentration camps' prisoners, and millions of forced labourers toiling in deadly conditions for his many departments, was beyond his sphere of knowledge. It was a hard-won image, which had convinced the Nuremberg judges, and satisfied the media; but it was an aura that would not stand the relentless and inquisitive test of time.

Following his release from Spandau in 1966, the media soon fell for his suave, gentlemanly, and plausible approach. Initially, his biographers in particular, and authors in general, all tended to give Speer the benefits of the many doubts surrounding his culpability as a war criminal. Over the two years I knew him as a prisoner in Spandau, we regularly talked about his 'guilt', and he admitted, on a number of occasions, knowing of, but not participating in, much that would embarrass Germany post-war. As a result of my personal and lengthy discussions with Speer, I believe his story is more straightforward than has generally been portrayed, I believe he was as guilty of war crimes as any Nazi but used his guile to survive. He openly revealed sufficient detail and information for me to believe he had successfully fooled the world into believing he was innocent of war crimes, even though, for fifteen years, he was constantly in the midst of Hitler's senior henchmen and at the forefront of German industry and production. His organisations used millions of slave labourers in grossly inhuman conditions, which he witnessed while on a number of project inspections. Due to his beguiling personality, Speer was spared the finality of the hangman's noose, but, by a quirk of judicial reasoning, and for reasons known only to the Nuremberg judges, the Allies perversely executed his deputy, Fritz Sauckel, for the crime of obeying Speer's orders.

Speer was a remarkable person; born to the wealthy German upper class he was clever, handsome with film star looks, polite, determined, his manners always correct, and a highly qualified architect. At the time of his trial he was described as 'hardly a German', which indicated a determination by a sufficient number of international prosecutors to willingly distance Speer from the other prisoners.[5] These were also qualities much admired by Hitler, who, having himself been labelled by the art world of the time as a failed and inconsequential artist, revelled in the company of someone seemingly clever and personable like Speer.

To understand Speer, this account falls into three parts: The first considers the early life and phenomenal success of the young Albert Speer until his imprisonment for war crimes in 1946. The second briefly traces my path to Spandau Prison as a freshly appointed British Army second lieutenant. The third part deals with my regular prison discussions with Speer, all noted at the time, and considers his attitude to, variously, Adolf Hitler, the Second World War, his understandings and beliefs at the time, and his avowed claim not to have known of the crimes for which he was prosecuted at Nuremberg. During our conversations, I endeavoured to get Speer's views on as many aspects of his life as he would permit, especially those of a political and personal nature. He particularly surprised me with his persistent denial of knowledge of the holocaust, yet was prepared to discuss his long-term relationship with Eva Braun, and his perceptively cruel advice to the Americans on dealing with Japan – which they followed. I conclude with my personal assessment of Speer based upon years of reflection, my diary notes made at the time of our conversations, together with my later experiences as a consultant clinical psychologist, and police psychologist for twenty-five years.

Chapter One

The Role of Albert Speer: Germany and Berlin Between the World Wars

'Heerlos, Wehrlos, Ehrlos'.
(Disarmed, Defenceless, Dishonoured.)[1]

B y October 1918, the First World War was nearly over. Nevertheless, the German Admiralty's chief of staff, Reinhard Scheer, decided to make his own point, and without any authority launched a final strike against the Royal Navy blockading German North Sea ports. He saw the operation as a means of both restoring the German navy's reputation, and lifting the Royal Navy's blockade. German civilians were hungry, they had suffered a poor harvest and there were no workers to bring in the scant crops; the population was on the verge of starvation but somehow remained stoic. Scheer's order to engage the Royal Navy ended with the words:

> An honourable battle by the fleet – even if it should be a fight to the death to sow the seed of a new German fleet of the future. There can be no future for a fleet fettered by a dishonourable peace.[2]

The German fleet was ordered to sail from Kiel on 28 October. The sailors knew it was a suicide mission, and five times they collectively refused to sail. Over 1,000 sailors were arrested for mutiny as their actions successfully immobilised the fleet. Over the following days, the revolt spread across the country with civilians and sailors rioting in Bremen, Hamburg, Lubeck and Munich. Kaiser Wilhelm abdicated and fled the country, leaving Germany in chaos. The fleet stayed in port.

In November 1918, Albert Speer was 13 years old when the German war effort finally ceased due to increasing Allied successes and a collapse of German morale, both civilian and military. Germany had suffered 37 million casualties, including 9 million dead combatants. Matters were made worse by the 1919 world-wide influenza epidemic, which killed more

Germans than had died during the war. There appeared to be little hope for the surviving German people, who then faced severe poverty and disease, all made worse by the uncontrolled spread of tuberculosis and rickets. With the war won, the war-weary Allies were disinterested in German suffering, or German politics; the USA retreated back into its previous isolation from Europe, Russia experienced the Revolution and Stalin's purges, and Britain and France were exhausted and weakly concentrated on rebuilding their own economies. Germany and its people were effectively abandoned to their fate.

In the first four years following the First World War, the very existence of the German people remained precarious; even its nation status was unclear, as before 1918 Germany was a federal Empire composed of twenty-five federal states. Political leadership was weak and severe food shortages improved little. Many German civilians and ex-soldiers mistakenly expected life to return to pre-war normality following the struggles suffered during the First World War. The German government from 1919 to 1933, the period between the First World War and the rise of Nazi Germany, went initially from uncertain beginnings with domination in Bavaria and Munich by the communists, and progressed to a brief season of success followed in 1923 by a devastating depression; this ensured sufficient chaos to position Germany ready for the rise of the Austrian Adolf Hitler (1889–1945) and his growing Nazi Party.[3]

Hitler came on the scene by cunning, stealth and deploying his mesmeric charm. In 1913, and fearing being called up for service in the Austrian army, Hitler left Vienna, but on returning for a rare family visit to his mother he was arrested for draft avoidance and taken before a local court. On being medically examined to assess his fitness for duty, he was rejected on unknown medical grounds and discharged. Free of military liability he returned to Munich where, for reasons unknown, he joined the Bavarian Army. His induction into the Bavarian Army was most likely an error by army recruiters, and a later investigation by the authorities failed to determine how Hitler was allowed to enlist, having been previously medically rejected as physically unfit for military service. Nevertheless, finding himself on the Western Front, Hitler was twice decorated for bravery. He received the relatively common Iron Cross Second Class in 1914, and the Iron Cross First Class in 1918, an honour rarely given to a corporal. It is noteworthy that his second decoration was recommended by Lieutenant Hugo Gutmann, his Jewish regimental adjutant.

In 1919, Hitler joined the National Socialist German Worker's Party, the DNVP (*Deutschnationale Volkspartei*) group which promoted anti-Semitism and sought a restoration of the monarchy, together with a repeal of the hated Versailles peace treaty, which had seized Germany's financial assets, her overseas territories and colonies, and banned German re-militarisation. Hitler became the party leader in 1921 through his utter determination, emotional and captivating speeches. He proposed national pride, militarism, and a commitment to the people for a racially 'pure' Germany. Hitler condemned the Jews, exploiting anti-Semitic feelings, which had prevailed across Europe for centuries, even writing 'the final aim must be an uncompromising removal of Jews altogether'.[4] He changed the name of the party to the National Socialist German Workers' Party, called for short, the Nazi Party (or NSDAP). A year later, like a psychopathic God, Hitler became its official leader, adopting the title of *Führer* (leader).

Rise of the Nazi Party
Since the 1920s, much of Berlin and Munich had been under the sway of Russian-linked communist groups, to the extent that Berlin was known across Germany as 'Red Berlin', the name was adopted across the country by German communists. From Munich in southern Germany, Hitler sought to counter communist philosophy by promoting the 'good old days', a strong incentive for hungry war-weary Germans hankering after peace, which further appealed to the younger generation by speaking with utter conviction that the young would again find pride in being German. Indeed, in desperation, the people began turning to extremists for salvation, and there were two organisations that welcomed desperate or angry young men.

The SA and the SS

The *Schutzstaffel* SS
In 1925, Hitler established the *Schutzstaffel*, or protection group, otherwise known as the SS. The SS were initially created as Hitler's personal bodyguards although they would go on to police the entire Third Reich, and its subjugated countries.

Until 1929, the SS was a small sub-division of the SA, with approximately 300 members. In 1929, Heinrich Himmler took command of the organisation and expanded it dramatically. By 1933, the SS had 35,000 members. Criteria for membership of the SS was based on applicants' 'racial purity', blind obedience, and fanatical loyalty to Hitler.

The SS saw themselves as the ultimate defenders of the 'Aryan' race and Nazi ideology. They terrorized opponents and aimed to destroy any person or group that threatened this belief.

The *Sturmabteilung* SA

The Nazi Party's paramilitary organisation, the *Sturmabteilung*, or attack response group, was more commonly known as the SA. Formed in 1921, the organisation grew out of the unemployed and Freikorps groups of ex-military, and was known as 'Stormtroopers' or 'Brownshirts' due to their brown uniform as worn by Hitler. Violent and often disorderly, the SA was primarily responsible for the protection of leading Nazis and disrupting other political opponents' meetings; they had a free rein and local police were under orders to ignore their activities. If Hitler was to gain power democratically, he needed to somehow curb their violent activities, which alarmed the public, and set out to change their reputation. A new leader, Franz von Salomon, was recruited. Rather than the violent free rein the SA had previously enjoyed, Salomon was strict and gave the organisation a more defined role. The SA and SS were still symbols of fear, and both were used by the Nazi Party to terrify their opposition into subordination, then to eliminate them entirely, or scare people from supporting opponents.

In March 1923, the First World War fighter plane ace, Hermann Goering, became the leader of the SA, which then had about 3,000 members based in and around Munich. The SA's primary responsibilities were to serve as Hitler's personal security detail, to provide military support to enforce Hitler's orders, and prevent the functioning of opposing parties, all by whatever means necessary. An example was the SA's Munich Beer Hall *Putsch* (coup) of 9 November 1923. The *putsch* was an attempted coup in which Hitler unsuccessfully attempted to seize control of the Bavarian government. On 8 November, Hitler and his SA mob marched and seized the unoccupied Munich army headquarters and a local newspaper office. The *putsch* could have succeeded, but failed after Hitler left the beer hall to attend to other business. At dawn the following day, and believing in their unopposed success, about 3,000 *putsch* supporters, who were all well versed in murderous street battles between the Nazis and their opponents, marched into the centre of Munich, heading for the Bavarian defence ministry to meet up with Hitler.

Meanwhile, the city police brought in army reinforcements, and from behind a barricade, met the advancing Nazis at close range with well-aimed rifle fire. Sixteen members of the SA died from the engagement and four police officers were killed during some vicious hand-to-hand fighting. Hitler fled having suffered a dislocated shoulder, but was arrested two days later to be charged with other Nazi leaders, including General Ludendorff and Rudolf Hess, with high treason, and sentenced to five years imprisonment; the NSDAP was banned, which led to the formal dissolution of the SA.

Hitler was released from prison after one year. It was while he was in prison that he wrote *Mein Kampf* (My Struggle), aided by his secretary, soon to be his deputy, the nationally famous pilot, Rudolf Hess. The SA members who died became revered as 'martyrs' in party mythology.

While Hitler was imprisoned and Goering hiding in exile, Hitler's longtime friend, Captain Ernst Röhm, an adventurer who had supported Hitler over the suspicious death of Hitler's young niece and flat-mate, Geli Raubal. Röhm continued organizing the disparate but sympathetic paramilitary groups, persuading them to join the SA under an umbrella organisation, known as the *Frontbann*. This was nothing more than a reorganized *Sturmabteilung*, created to replace the SA, which had been banned in the aftermath of the failed Munich *putsch*. In February 1925, the *Frontbann* was dissolved after the ban on the SA was lifted. It was in 1930 that Albert Speer first came on the scene, when he attended a Hitler speech in Berlin. The following day he joined the Nazi Party, and, as a result, found work with senior Nazi officials in Berlin. Röhm became chief of staff of the SA in 1931, and to strengthen Röhm's position, Hitler made him his personal chief of staff. By 1932, the SA had grown to 400,000 members. Just two years later, Hitler was named chancellor while the SA's numbers swelled to over 3 million, some ten times larger than the German Army. Speer was now working as Hitler's personal architect, while, at the same time, there were tens of thousands of dissatisfied young men without work, without money, and without a purpose. The Nazis rewarded Speer with a top position, while the SA gave the young rebels a cause.

The Nazi Party was not yet in the position to overthrow the state, but it was getting progressively closer by infiltrating government departments and plotting to bring the police and army under their control. There was no national German police force; policing was haphazard and regional, which presented the Nazis with an easy opportunity to consolidate law enforcement under the Nazi Party. Hitler tasked a team with special responsibility for police standardisation; its leader was a senior Nazi, Heinrich Himmler, assisted by an up-and-coming junior Nazi, Reinhard Heydrich, a Hitler fanatic with an overt anti-Semitic attitude.[5]

Under orders from Hitler's officials, the SA played a major part in the Nazis' increasing public popularity by taking firm action to repress dissidents; its backbone consisted largely of violent anti-leftist and anti-democratic former soldiers who were only too enthusiastic to lend their muscle to the growing Nazi Party. With a strict form of internal discipline to encourage obedience, and brutality to opponents, they acquired the nickname 'Brownshirts', copied from the shirt worn in public by Hitler. As the auxiliary police body, they practised repressive terror against anyone they chose. No one was safe, especially opponents, political or otherwise, and groups such as the Jews. Their acts and behaviour were protected by law; they had the protection of the civil police and military to behave as thugs of the worst kind against whosoever they chose to treat as criminals; many victims had already been secretly condemned to death before their victims even knew they were in trouble. Anyone who questioned the arrival or purpose of the SA, usually at night, could be severely beaten, while those targeted for elimination were either murdered on the spot or taken off, never to be seen again. The rationale behind their legal brutality was to publicise their savage punishment of opponents in order to terrorise the German public into submission; it also silenced any opposition, or the mentioning of widespread public fear of the situation. The SA encouraged the willingness of Germans to settle old scores by rewarding those denouncing friends and neighbours; such denunciations gave every citizen the power to 'get even' with whosoever they chose, and such malevolence was rewarded by the SA. Hitler Youth children were part of Nazi intelligence gathering, with party officials regularly completing questionnaires at youth camps and meetings designed to reveal details of parents, relatives or school teachers who might have opined against the party. This is understandable when remembering the Hitler Youth slogan was 'We are born to die for Germany'.

Although he was fast becoming a leading politician, until January 1933 Hitler was never approved of by the majority of Germans to become their leader. His power base was in the eastern half of Germany, whereas just 17 per cent of voters in the predominately Catholic west ever voted for him. Then, after a brief struggle for power, and when public elections failed to produce a leading party, President Paul von Hindenburg resorted to appointing Hitler as the new German chancellor.

With Hitler now controlling the German parliament, the Reichstag, opposition members became powerless when they were refused access to the building by members of the SA. Hitler had total control and there were no more debates, unless Hitler wished to pronounce. Within weeks, nearly 100 Reichstag members disappeared or died, with nearly 200 exiled from Germany. Hitler then invoked totalitarian laws to quash civil rights and suppress members of the Communist Party. Goering increased police strength with 40,000 thugs from the SA and SS authorised police to fire on gatherings of political opponents. In February, the Reichstag building was destroyed by fire, undoubtedly organised by the Nazis themselves, giving them the excuse to unleash the mass and frequently brutal arrest of detractors, especially Communists.

In March 1933, when Albert Speer was 28 years old and well established on Hitler's staff, Hitler introduced the 'Enabling Act' to allow him to pass laws without the approval of Germany's parliament or president, and stated it was 'the new German kingdom of greatness and power and glory and justice. Amen'.[6] 'Amen' would shortly become *Sieg Heil*!

During 1933, one effect of Nazis' suppression of all other political parties was the construction by the SS of concentration camps across Germany. Camp staffs were encouraged by their senior officers, who, having been specially trained at the Dachau camp, began enforcing a widespread in human policy of instilling fear and practising brutality towards inmates. Prisoners could be shot, but guards were reminded that each bullet cost two pfennigs (a farthing). Alternatively, prisoners could be hanged, beaten and tortured at will without question. These pre-war camps were successful at removing Nazi Party antagonists from society. If and when such unfortunates survived to reach the end of their sentences, those still considered 'dangerous' were placed in 'protective custody' and detained in lunatic asylums or murdered in concentration camps. These early camps were indeed brutal beyond belief, but they were not yet supporting the transfer of prisoners to the mass extermination camps that would follow. The press were encouraged to report certain executions under the guise of the victims having been criminals, which the public tended to believe and accept for the benefit of the greater good. With the belief established that these camps served a useful purpose in German society, inmates were widely forced to work in industry and were moved around in full view of the public. Hitler still lacked public support and something was needed to swing public opinion in favour of the Nazis.

How Hitler and the Nazi Party rose to power
In the nine years between 1924 and 1933, the Nazi Party transformed from a small, violent, revolutionary party to the largest elected party in the Reichstag. Whilst Hitler was in prison, following the Munich *putsch* in 1923, Alfred Rosenberg took over as temporary leader of the Nazi Party. Rosenberg was an ineffective leader, and the party became divided over key issues. The failure of the Munich *putsch* had shown Hitler that he would not be able to take power by force. Hitler therefore decided to change tactics and instead focus on winning support for his party democratically, then being elected to power. Following his release from prison on 20 December 1924, Hitler convinced the chancellor of Bavaria to remove the ban on the Nazi Party.

In February 1926, Hitler restructured the Nazi Party to make it more efficient. Firstly, the Nazi Party adopted a new framework, which divided Germany into regions called *Gaue*. Each *Gau* had its own leader, a *Gauleiter*. Each *Gau* was then divided into subsections, called *Kreise*. Each *Kreis* had its own leader, called a *Kreisleiter*. Each *Kreis* was then divided into even smaller sections, each with its own leader, and so on. Each of these sections, usually a town or village, was responsible to the section above them, with Hitler at the very top of the party and having ultimate authority. The Nazis also established new affiliated groups for different professions, from children, to teachers, doctors, and to lawyers. These groups were encouraged to infiltrate the already existing social structures, and help the party gain more members and supporters. These political changes transformed the Nazi Party from a paramilitary organisation focused on overthrowing the republic by force, to one focused on gaining power through elections and popular support.

Röhm and Hitler both desired a strong Germany. As a former soldier wounded three times during the First World War, Röhm was especially upset that the German defeat had resulted in strict limitations on the country's military. He believed the German army should be large, fierce, and steadfast. Like Hitler, Röhm was also ruthless. His only weakness would manifest itself later when underestimating the Führer's wrath whenever he was challenged. Meanwhile, Röhm and Hitler grew stronger; both felt Germany needed to control its own destiny. Together, they decided to take increasingly drastic actions to change Germany.

As head of the SA, Röhm now commanded a sizeable force that could take over at any time, but he lacked Hitler's diplomatic skills. There was no control over Röhm's SA activities, which invariably featured violence and disorder. He was tremendously powerful among Hitler's rank and file, and was certainly a favourite of Hitler. To have some control over Röhm, Hitler brought him into his cabinet – without portfolio. Röhm's personality was overwhelming; he was the only senior Nazi who would deliberately refer to Hitler by his first name, as opposed to the usual *Mein Führer.* Worse, Röhm was openly gay, which was then illegal, to which Hitler appeared to turn a blind eye. As the SA grew, the organisation continued to embrace violence by aggressively interfering with the meetings of opposing political parties, fighting in the streets with other paramilitaries, influencing elections, and intimidating Jews, Roma, Communists, and Social Democrats; all groups they believed were 'enemies of Germany'. Cases of political intimidation were widespread; in March 1933 the Königsburg SA ransacked the office of the regional Social Democrats, beat one of the delegates to death, and then, with the staff held in custody, openly tortured several distraught office staff to gain information and confessions about their colleagues' activities. In Wuppertal, eight SA members fell upon the ex-bandleader of a well-known Communist music group as he walked home one night, shooting him dead.

Under Ernst Röhm, the SA not only grew, but also became much better organised, if not endowed with much foresight or clear vision. Once Hitler came to power, Röhm formulated a secret plan for the *Sturmabteilung* to absorb and replace the German military, a highly controversial concept, which would strongly antagonise senior military officers. Röhm was a totally committed Nazi, whose beliefs were motivated more by ideological discipline than personal devotion to Hitler. Once Hitler became chancellor in January 1933, the strength, size, and brutality of the SA, especially under Röhm's leadership, meant the SA was a potential liability within the fledgling Nazi state, and now posed a challenge to Hitler's consolidation of power. Even after the Nazi seizure of power, SA violence continued across Germany. Oddly, at Speer's suggestion, Hitler insisted that as many SA events as possible should be held at night, both to give greater prominence to Speer's lighting effects and to hide the protruding flesh of the corpulent *Sturmabteilung*, who had become glaringly overweight during the recent years from the fruits of their plunder.

By the end of 1941, Hitler had tired of hearing that the SA, SS and police had protected known homosexuals in their ranks, he authorised an extraordinary order that homosexuals in these services would be executed. Accordingly, a passage was inserted into SA, SS and police disciplinary procedures requiring homosexual members to be executed. It is not known if, or how rigorously, this policy was enforced.

The Reichstag fire

On 31 January 1933, Hitler, conscious of his lack of a majority in the Reichstag, called for new elections to try to strengthen his position. The Nazis aimed to increase their share of the vote so that they would gain a majority in the Reichstag, allowing them to rule unopposed, and unhindered by rival parties, or coalition governments. Over the next two months they launched themselves into an intense election campaign. The Nazis were violently opposed to the Communist Party, their main opponents, who believed the private ownership of land and assets was theft. It was a policy that led Germany's rich landowners and businessmen to support the Nazis. With such support, the SA began attacking communist meetings. On 27 February, precisely four weeks after Hitler was sworn in as chancellor of Germany, the campaign moved into its final, frantic days. The Reichstag, the main German Parliament building in Berlin, was set on fire and burnt down; Hitler's propaganda minister, Joseph Goebbels, is believed to have orchestrated the fire to elicit public sympathy. Certainly, an atmosphere of public fear followed the fire, and the Nazis used the growing public unease to their advantage, encouraging widespread anti-communist sentiment. Goering falsely declared that the Communists had planned a national uprising to overthrow the Weimar Republic. This added to the hysteria, turning the public further against the Communists, and resulted in some 4,000 of them being arrested. The Communist Party was promptly banned and Nazi opponents were brutally suppressed. In one ferocious night 1,500 communist functionaries were arrested across Germany, with most never to be seen again. This action put paid to the Communist campaign planned for the forthcoming March elections.

The day after the fire, Hindenburg signed an emergency decree for the 'Protection of the German People'. Public unease improved with the highly publicised arrest and trial of a young Dutch communist, Marinus van der Lubbe, who had originally agreed to participate in the conspiracy in exchange for money and a rail ticket home, but, to ensure secrecy, the Nazis reneged on their agreement, and instead executed him by guillotine at Leipzig Prison. Four weeks later, Adolf Hitler was sworn in as chancellor of Germany. The violence continued and in June 1933, an event known as the 'Köpenick blood-week' caused widespread concern. A confrontation between Social Democrats and the SA had resulted in the deaths of three Storm Troopers; in a savage response, the SA arrested more than 500 men; beatings and torture ensued, with 91 deaths. Röhm and his violent Stormtroopers were now causing widespread public concern, as well as becoming too powerful for Hitler's liking.

Biding his time did not improve matters, and a year later Hitler came under even greater pressure. There was a strong growing awareness of the mutual dislike between the traditional conservative elites of Germany, representing those within industry, the churches, politics and business; many of whom maintained key positions in the government and the army during the first years of the Third Reich. Most supported Hitler, but engaged in infighting between themselves to gain power. Even with Hitler being elected chancellor, little changed. Röhm and the SA were still keen to continue their 'revolution' and replace the traditional conservative elite with their own. Hitler and his senior Nazi leadership disagreed with Röhm's brash approach and collectively understood the need to appear moderate. Their plan was to take over slowly by stealth, and, where possible, democratic means, not by violent force. This required maintaining the stability and illusion of a democracy; the tension between the SA and the Nazi leadership continued to fester and grow.

Worryingly for Hitler, Röhm's SA now numbered over 3 million, and Röhm had mildly jested that he could easily unseat Hitler by sheer force of numbers. Further, many senior Nazis were developing a strong dislike of Röhm, an overt and brash homosexual leading an out-of-control mob, and they knew his presence as a senior Nazi was already reflecting poorly on Hitler's standing with the people.

Röhm's overt ambition to merge the army with his SA was seriously worrying not only to Hitler but to the German military's high command. The *Reichswehr*, the established German military, had long despised Röhm, and they let it be known that they would fiercely object to any merger. Hitler came under growing pressure to act, and on 28 February 1934 he informed the army high command that they were in charge, not Röhm. Piqued, Röhm pointedly made his objections known to Hitler and openly began to query Hitler's policy. On 20 April, a suspicious and wary Goering ordered Röhm's telephone calls to be monitored; he then transferred control of the Prussian political police (*Gestapo*) to Himmler, who, Goering believed, could be relied upon to act on Hitler's instructions against Röhm. Plans were prepared to eliminate Röhm. Speer, as a member of Hitler's inner circle, was present at these secret meetings, only to later deny he had ever heard of Röhm. Himmler appointed his deputy, Reinhard Heydrich, a family friend of Röhm who had recently been Godfather to Heydrich's youngest child, to lead the Gestapo action. There was to be no mercy for the unsuspecting Röhm.

Röhm seemed to enjoy playing with fire by maintaining the ongoing talk of a 'second revolution' to entrench National Socialism, which seriously alarmed Hitler. This fear was intensified by the powerful anti-Röhm faction of Goering and Himmler, who fed false information to Hitler, cleverly collated by Heydrich, claiming that Röhm was actively planning a leadership challenge against Hitler. The threat of an imminent Röhm coup finally succeeded in turning Hitler against him. By June 1934 these tensions came to a head and resulted in a violent and typical Hitler solution. On 28 June, Hitler, having for so long been reluctant to act against Röhm, struck first. He ordered the unsuspecting Röhm to assemble some eighty-five of his top SA leaders for a conference at a luxury spa in Bad Wiessee, near Munich. The trap was set; Heydrich launched the purge of the SA.

Between 30 June and 2 July 1934, The Night of the Long Knives, or 'Operation Hummingbird', also known as the Röhm *putsch*, was carried out primarily by the SS and Heydrich's Gestapo. The operation was well planned, using weapons and trucks supplied by army headquarters. The aim was to neutralise Röhm and purge the SA leadership, and other influential political opponents – all in one fell swoop. The SA had long been a critical component of Hitler's rise to power, but now Hitler feared the SA under Röhm's dynamic leadership was becoming a serious threat to his own leadership.

At about 4.30 am on 30 June 1934, Hitler and his SS entourage secretly arrived by air in Munich. From the airport they drove in convoy to the Bavarian Interior Ministry, where they knew the city's senior police officers and local SA leaders were assembled following a particularly violent rampage that had, by chance, taken place in the city's streets earlier that night; it had been orchestrated by the SA while the police looked on. On arriving at the Ministry, Hitler was briefed about the orgy of violence, which had only just subsided; an enraged shouting Hitler went to the office of the chief of Munich police, *Obergruppenführer* Schneidhuber, and tore the epaulettes off the police chief's shirt, while accusing him of failing to keep order in the city, and of treachery. Schneidhuber was beaten to the floor, and then dragged away to be executed later that day, along with the other SA leaders. As the tired and bemused *Sturmabteilung* were hustled off to prison, Hitler led his specialist group of SS to the Hanselbauer Hotel in nearby Bad Wiessee, where Röhm and his followers were staying.

Hitler arrived at the hotel just after 6.00 am. The SA leadership, still in bed, were taken by complete surprise. SS men stormed through the hotel, arresting the confused high-ranking SA leaders, while Hitler personally placed the bemused Röhm under arrest. The SS found Breslau SA leader, Edmund Heines, in bed with an unidentified 18-year-old male SA trooper. A furious Hitler ordered both Heines and his partner to be taken outside the hotel where they were shot. Goebbels emphasized this homosexual aspect in subsequent propaganda by justifying the purge as a crackdown on moral turpitude. Hitler's *Leibstandarte* then ferried the arrested men to Stadelheim Prison; there in the prison courtyard, the *Leibstandarte* firing squad went to work. Their victims included five SA generals and an SA colonel. Those not immediately executed were taken back to the *Leibstandarte* barracks for questioning before being shot by firing squad.

Meanwhile, that morning at Munich railway station, other unsuspecting senior SA leaders had arrived by special train for their planned meeting with Röhm and Hitler, only to be unceremoniously collected together and arrested before they left the station. Taken under armed guard to the *Leibstandarte* barracks, they were given one-minute 'trials' and shot in batches by the SS firing squad. Röhm was offered the choice of suicide or death; he refused both. Following lunch, Hitler ordered two SS leaders, Theodor Eicke, commandant of the Dachau concentration camp, and his SS adjutant, Michael Lippert, to execute Röhm. On entering Röhm's cell, they handed him a Browning pistol loaded with a single bullet and gave him ten minutes to shoot himself – or they would do it for him. Röhm demurred, telling them, 'If I am to be killed, let Adolf do it himself.' Having heard nothing in the allotted time, they returned to Röhm's cell at 2.50 pm to find him standing, with his bare chest puffed out in a gesture of defiance; Eicke and Lippert both shot Röhm.

In the following days, a further 200 senior SA officers were tracked down and arrested before being shot by the SS firing squads. Armed with pre-arranged lists of remaining senior SA officers, Heydrich's SS squads in Berlin arrested every senior SA officer; none survived. Buoyed up by his success, Hitler now seized the day and ordered Himmler to unleash the Gestapo against old enemies, from lowly press reporters to top politicians, such as Kurt von Schleicher, a former general and Hitler's predecessor as chancellor, together with his wife. Both were murdered at their home just for being wary of Hitler. Others killed included Gregor Strasser, a former senior Nazi who had angered Hitler by resigning from the party in 1932, and Gustav Ritter von Kahr, the former Bavarian state commissioner who ordered the crushing of the Beer Hall *Putsch* in 1923. Kahr's actions had infuriated Hitler, and his body was found in a wood outside Munich; he had been hacked to death, apparently with pickaxes. Fritz Gerlich disappeared, a journalist who had raised a number of embarrassing questions when he investigated the death of Geli Raubal, Hitler's niece and alleged mistress. Erich Klausener, president of the Catholic Action movement, who had regularly queried Hitler's motives, was also shot. Hitler had no time for Catholicism, he wrote in *Mein Kampf*: 'The Catholic Church was not in sympathy with the German people but… supported their adversaries.'

Those murdered included several accidental and curious victims: one was Willi Schmid, a popular and well-known music critic of the *Münchner Neueste Nachrichten* newspaper, but who unfortunately shared the same name as a Hitler opponent. Over the next few days, his wife made furious protests to the press, which resulted in Rudolf Hess visiting her, and buying her silence by awarding her a substantial widow's pension. Another outstanding issue for Hitler was also resolved that night; the owner of Röhm's favourite Munich restaurant, the *Bratwurst Glockl*, and his manager, Herr Zehnter, were also arrested and shot. On the evening before Geli's suicide, Hitler and Geli had been dining at the restaurant and their presence and behaviour was witnessed by the ever-attentive restaurant owner. By eliminating Zehntner, the possible reasons for Geli Raubal's death would remain unexplained and deter any further speculation. As Himmler's adjutant, Karl Wolff, later explained, friendship and personal loyalty were not allowed to stand in the way, stating: 'Bodies were found in fields and woods for weeks afterwards and files of petitions from relatives of the missing remained active for months. What seems certain is that, with Hitler's intervention, less than half were SA officers.'

Following the coup, a telegram was sent to Hitler by the ailing President Hindenburg, Germany's highly revered military hero, expressing his 'profoundly felt gratitude', and congratulating Hitler for 'nipping treason in the bud'. Goering later commented during the Nuremberg trials that the Hindenburg telegram had been prepared and sent by the Nazis. Hindenburg also announced that the army was the 'sole bearer of arms', and that the military were not obliged to join the Nazi Party. Senior army officers, who had been disparagingly referred to as 'old clods' by Röhm, now applauded the coup, even though former Generals Kurt von Schleicher and Ferdinand von Bredow were among the victims of the murderers. On receiving the news of the coup, the army high command sent Hitler a message which was immediately published in the German press, stating that 'the army stands behind Adolf Hitler, who remains one of ours' and promptly swore personal allegiance to Hitler. With agreement between the Nazi regime and the German Army (*Reichswehr*), Hitler could now proclaim himself Führer of National Socialist Germany, and claim absolute power. Writing to the British ambassador to Germany, Sir Eric Phipps, the consul general in Munich, St Clair Gainer, wrote:

> The feeling amongst the *Reichswehr* officers is that Hitler has given the army back its self-respect, and the army are therefore prepared to co-operate with him provided he will to some extent modify his socialist programme and keep his followers and minor chieftains in proper subjection. PRO 371/17708.

Whilst the coup focused on the SA, the Nazis had also used the opportunity to eliminate other political opponents. Among those killed by the SS between 30 June and 2 July were Schleicher's friend and collaborator, Major General Ferdinand von Bredow, and Gregor Strasser, a former Nazi leader, who, in the winter of 1932, had sought to reach an electoral agreement with the then Chancellor von Schleicher, an agreement that would have barred Hitler from rising to power. The SS also targeted von Papen, Hitler's political deputy, who had fallen out of favour with Hitler; he was arrested in his own office and somehow managed to escape with his life but not before they frightened the old man into silence by killing two of his senior aides in front of him, Edgar Jung and Herbert von Bose; their crime was to write a less-than-endearing speech about Hitler for von Papen.

Meanwhile, following the coup, Goebbels engineered the country's media to present the event as a necessary preventative measure, in response to the SA's 'plan to overthrow the government'. As the SA was well-known for being violent and unruly, many saw this as a legitimate move by the government to ensure public order; the rule of the mob had to be seen by the public as having failed. Hitler and the Nazi Party were then able to consolidate their position of having absolute power in Germany by quietly removing all political opposition. The mass murder of SA leaders was also intended to improve the image of Hitler's government with a German public that had become increasingly critical of thuggish SA tactics. In all, surviving Nazi sources initially identified by name eighty-five senior persons killed in the Röhm purge; the actual toll of the purge was estimated by the world's press to be well beyond 500 victims.

On 3 July 1934, the Reich Cabinet proposed a backdated law to legalise the purge arrests and mass murders as an emergency action to save the nation. Hitler addressed the Reichstag on 13 July, explaining that as the supreme ruler of Germany he had exercised his power against individuals who threatened the very existence of the German nation. The Reichstag retrospectively approved a bill legalising the coup, and the following purge, as emergency defence measures. Speer now became heavily involved; he was commissioned to design and oversee the extension of the 'Italianate Palais' located next to the chancellery, even though it was occupied by Hitler's vice chancellor, the out-of-favour von Papen. On Hitler's orders, von Papen was further humiliated by being evicted from his office. Arriving at the building, Speer was horrified to see pools of congealed blood and stains left after the murder of von Papen's secretary, Herbert von Bose, following the Röhm *putsch*. The building was to be the new headquarters for the SA, to be moved on Hitler's order from Munich to Berlin so as to be more easily controlled.

On 20 July, Hitler decreed the SS were, then and there, independent of the SA as reward for their loyalty and role in carrying out the purge. This granted SS *Reichsführer* Himmler direct access to Hitler, and gave a distinct advantage to the SS in realising its ambition to gain control of the German police. Now completely leaderless, the SA was forcibly reduced in size, dropping by 40 per cent to 1.8 million and losing most of its power to the SS. During the second half of 1934, the SS assumed control of a centralized political police force and concentration camp system.

The widespread murder of political opponents had now been made almost acceptable, although not everyone in high places was happy with recent events. The former Kaiser, Wilhelm II, who was in exile at Doorn in the Netherlands, was horrified by the purges. He asked, 'What would people have said if I had done such a thing?' Hearing of the murder by the SS of the former Chancellor Kurt von Schleicher and his wife, just for openly speaking against the Nazis, he commented: 'We have ceased to live under the rule of law and everyone must be prepared for the possibility that the Nazis will push their way in and put them up against the wall!'

On the 28 December 1934, the *Daily Mail* commented under the headline 'Germany on her feet again':

What magic has restored hope to German hearts?... given to German eyes the flash of courage and self-confidence, and magnetised this mighty nation until one feels in its midst as if one were in a gigantic power-house. Hitler. That is the answer.

Speer and Röhm

In his book, *Inside the Third Reich* (1970), Speer pointed out, 'After 1933 there quickly formed various rival factions that held divergent views, spied on each other, and held each other in contempt.' And although a full member of Hitler's inner circle, Speer later denied any knowledge of Röhm or the Röhm *putsch*. Yet the following purge of Röhm's senior officer corps was a dramatic national event and was especially well-known among Hitler's top Nazis; it had sent ripples of fear through the remaining echelons of the SA, especially as it resulted in mass arrests and executions across Germany. The event was widely publicized in the German and World press, yet Speer hardly mentioned the event in his book, merely commenting that Hindenburg had approved of the initial *putsch*, and following purge, which Speer found 'highly reassuring'. He wrote, 'with such arguments we soothed our consciences'. By professing not to know about the *putsch*, or its brutal aftermath, Speer followed his favoured and comfortable line of 'being there but not knowing', which he used so successfully at his Nuremberg trial, and after his release, to perpetuate this defence.

When interviewed by Gitta Sereny for her book, *Albert Speer: His Battle with Truth*, Speer commented on the resulting purge: 'When it was actually happening, of course one could hardly avoid being aware... as the streets were full of soldiers and there was a crisis atmosphere. And as I saw Hitler every day I knew he was perturbed.'

Due to his senior ministerial position, there is little doubt that Speer would have been in the midst of the very intensive and secretive planning to eliminate Röhm; however, during our conversations, Speer claimed not to have known anything about the Röhm *putsch*, or to have met or known of Reinhard Heydrich, who led the Gestapo action against Röhm. However, according to another researcher, Heydrich was well-known to Speer who was awaiting a visit from Speer to redesign the city of Prague to Heydrich's own specifications, which were along the same architectural lines as Speer's proposed new Berlin. A joint meeting was in the process of being arranged for the pair to discuss plans in Prague, so it is improbable that Speer knew nothing about Heydrich. In a similar vein, Speer's detailed work *Inside the*

Third Reich gives the Reichstag fire scant mention; although this fine and famous national building in the centre of Berlin was thereafter abandoned as a ruin, for an architect of Speer's stature, not easily overlooked.[7]

Now known as the SD, the *Sicherheitsdienst*, Heydrich's growing intelligence service was based on the British secret service system, which he had long admired. Staffed by like-minded and ambitious young middle-class men, it was established as the Nazi national security system, with Heydrich's intention of eventually making himself 'all powerful' for intelligence, firstly under Himmler then Hitler. At Heydrich's insistence, the demoralised SA was deliberately placed under the control of a weak official, and had any remaining authority or original thought removed. Heydrich was only interested in State security and now sought Hitler's authority to build, and control, every aspect of German intelligence network. In June 1936, Himmler was appointed chief of German police, with Heydrich head of the Gestapo, the *Geheime Staatspolizei* or Secret State Police. Heydrich had long been focused against the Jews and other groups, such as criminals, alcoholics and those unable to find work, who soon found themselves in concentration camps. During the early war years, Heydrich sought control of all concentration camps.[8]

The *putsch* and following murders were not considered at the Nuremberg Tribunal because the court's remit was solely to consider matters which had taken place since the commencement of the Second World War. This also explains why the appalling atrocities committed in 1936 by German troops in Spain's civil war were also beyond the Tribunal's jurisdiction or remit.

Hindenburg's death

In the meantime, on 2 August 1934, President Hindenburg died; he was 87. Shortly afterwards, Hitler announced that the two offices of the chancellor and president were to be combined to create one position, of *Führer*, with all the powers of the former chancellor. Hitler announced that he would occupy this new role. On 19 August 1934, the German people were asked to vote on whether or not they approved of the merging of the two offices with Hitler's new *Führer* role; 95.7 per cent of the population voted, 89.93 per cent in favour of Hitler.

With Hindenburg gone there was no longer a limit to Hitler's power. He had effortlessly moved from being chancellor to dictator. Within weeks, Berlin's newspaper stands displayed the Nazi flag, with passers-by required to salute the flag with the 'Heil' salute. Everyone obliged; the alternative was an immediate beating from SA thugs, now aligned with Hitler.

A few weeks later, churches across Berlin were ordered to fly the swastika flag.[9] Within days the flags were everywhere to be seen: outside shops, on street corners, in cafes and on public transport. On special Nazi occasions, houses and flats were expected to be swathed in swastika flags, non-compliance was rare because failure to comply brought the wrath of neighbours fearful of being reported by other neighbours. Nazi Brownshirts appeared to be on every street corner, ensuring respect. For normal people it was life in a confusing madhouse, and it was about to get worse, much worse. The Nazis' intention was to create a single German community that would make religion or social class irrelevant, it became known as the *Volksgemeinschaft* (people's community), which Germans quickly accepted as being the new Germany.

German civilians would later maintain that, within their own families and homes, life pre-war still had a semblance of normality, while agreeing that they would happily attend Nazi parades, meetings, work seminars and give friends and colleagues the 'Heil Hitler' salute, a compulsory greeting which extended to every office including the civil courts. Employees and managers complied with the decree from the Nazi Labour Front leader, Dr Robert Ley, to wear a blue uniform; this was the required garment to be worn by both workers and supervisors in work. By copying the example of their 'ex-worker' the *Führer*, every German could now believe they were becoming part of the 'master class'. Ever one of the people, Hitler would remind the Germans that he toiled only for the German people, and pointed out that he was alone among politicians in not having a bank account or owning any shares. He never admitted his secret substantial income from copyrighting his image on every German postage stamp, or from royalties amassed by the sale of his popular *Mein Kampf*, with a special copy presented to each couple on their wedding day, paid for by central government funds.

At the same time, open anti-Semitism had become accepted across Germany, with widespread humiliation and public attacks on Jews. This vile harassment, described in the German press as 'heroic', climaxed on the 9 November 1938 with *Kristallnacht*, the 'Night of Broken Glass' as it became known. Propaganda Minister Joseph Goebbels initiated this violent free-for-all against the Jews, during which nearly 1,000 synagogues were set on fire and 100 destroyed. More than 7,000 Jewish businesses and homes were looted and wrecked, several hundred Jews were killed trying to defend their property, and, in the days that followed, a further 30,000 Jews were rounded up and sent to concentration camps to be tormented, placed into forced labour or murdered. This brutal action was quietly tolerated by the German people, who had become aware of Nazi mythology that Jews transmitted disease and were their enemy, and had therefore become apathetic to their plight. Lowly officials in positions of power were well placed to bribe Jews for their life savings, just to be temporarily removed from deportation 'lists'. Likewise, those officials responsible for the issue of essential permits and ration books made small fortunes from Jews who could still afford to be bribed. The people appeared to be indifferent to the growing plight of German Jews and equally indifferent to the mass deportations, almost to the point of Germans being subconsciously silenced by what they saw happening around them, and therefore acquiescing to events. And they were powerless to voice an opposing opinion against the party line, even if they wanted to; every citizen was vulnerable to be informed against, rendering them liable to the feared Gestapo 'tap on the shoulder' for stepping out of line.

Since 1932, the Nazis had promoted their cause and actions by taking control of the national press and radio, and in March 1933, Goebbels was placed in charge of the media, with the licence fees being diverted to Goebbels' Ministry of Propaganda. Nazi propaganda was pervasive and incessant and controlled the news, media, arts and information across Germany. Goebbels had made rapid progress in the party; he joined the Nazi Party in 1924 and in 1926 was appointed *Gauleiter* (district leader) for Berlin, where he oversaw the use of propaganda to promote the Nazi Party and its programme. From 1934 onwards, and with Hitler now supreme, Goebbels' propaganda was the only news the German population could readily access. He was particularly adept at using radio and film for propaganda purposes; radio ownership was encouraged and increased nationally from 4 to 16 million. For those without radios, huge loudspeakers were erected in public spaces at over 6,000 major public spaces across Berlin and Germany. Special official radio announcements were considered so important that, during their broadcast, office staff were subjected to silence by 'wireless wardens' and people near public loudspeakers were required by the SA to stand still and listen. Newspapers were less important as few had a worthwhile circulation. In any event, these were soon taken over by Goebbels, who had an eye on redirecting advertising revenue to his ministry. By 1937, Himmler completed the consolidation of all German police forces under SS control, and excluded the police from any form of legal or judicial supervision.

Now freed by law to do as they wished, the Gestapo and SA began arresting the remaining Communist leaders, prominent Jews, socialists and dissenting labour dignitaries. They were removed to overcrowded locations including breweries, factories, barracks and ships, where they were subjected to progressive dehumanisation by being shorn and put into striped pyjama-type clothes. Beatings and torture were ritual and few victims were ever seen again. In Berlin alone, the SA and SS recorded over a hundred such holding locations; meanwhile concentration camps were being developed and enlarged. In the end, there were hundreds of such camps spread across Germany, most were designed and built by Speer's departments, and many were near cities, towns and villages, which complicates the question of not only Speer's, but the whole German population's alleged lack of knowledge of such camps.

For the Jews, they knew full well that their lives were increasingly in jeopardy; of the thousand most qualified German Jewish academics, nearly a quarter emigrated by 1933. Jewish property was constantly being vandalised or expropriated by looters and officials. Jews were openly harassed in the streets by roaming SA gangs, and most Jews lost their jobs. Then they were barred from public office, and places such as cinemas, and even banned from swimming in public pools and rivers for fear of polluting the water. Jewish children were barred from attending school; Jews had to forfeit their German nationality, and were forbidden to marry or have relationships with 'Aryans'. This relationship decree caused great confusion to both administrators and the Jewish people, as it then had to be decided who was a full Jew, and who was partially Jewish, or descendants from grandparents, or even great-grandparents.

Within days of the brutality of *Kristallnacht*, the Nazis forced all professional Jews to transfer their businesses and property to Aryan hands and expelled all Jewish pupils from public schools. With brazen arrogance, the Nazis further persecuted the Jews by forcing them to pay for any damage caused to Jewish property by the mobs. As a senior minister attending Hitler's meetings, Speer would have been fully aware of the measures being taken against the Jews.

On 1 September 1939, Germany invaded Poland and sent the Luftwaffe to bomb Warsaw; 1,500 sorties were flown and the city was badly damaged. Two days later, Britain and France declared war on Germany. Germany was then in a strong position, with victory anywhere seemingly guaranteed. Hitler had no viable challengers either within or without Germany so Hitler, having quickly overcome Europe, and with Britain in a state of economic and military distress (except for the RAF), turned his attention towards Russia, a subject too well-known to require amplification in this account.

Chapter Two

Albert Speer: Hitler's Architect and Close Confidant During the Years 1931–1945

'A comfortable alibi for a whole new generation of Germans'[1]

As Hitler's Minister of Armaments and War Production in the Second World War, Speer proved to be one of the most important and influential men in Nazi Germany, and the most competent facilitator of the German economy and war effort as a whole. Until the final weeks of Hitler's Germany, Speer was totally committed to Hitler.

Between 1961 and 1963, towards the end of his twenty years' imprisonment in Berlin's notorious Spandau Prison, I was privileged to experience a number of extraordinary meetings and very private conversations with Speer. He would not be released until 1966. From the outset, Speer was both willing and enthusiastic to talk with me, perhaps due to my young age. During our meetings, I learned a lot from him, which I review in the following chapters, but I was fully aware that, notwithstanding his conviction at Nuremberg as a war criminal, I was uniquely placed to be able to regularly meet and talk with this infamous figure. To me, he was a figure of great interest and historical importance, having been one of the most powerful men in the Second World War; now this once-famous man was locked up year-after-year in a strictly run prison and was excruciatingly lonely. Yet, during this particular point in time, as a young army officer, he was regularly accessible to me, while remaining inaccessible to the rest of the world. I saw him for what he was, a highly intelligent prisoner living a harsh life behind bars, with no outside contact, and without access to any newspapers or news reports. Over a period of two years I would regularly talk with him and ask him numerous questions, and it is these questions and his answers which I noted at the time. We did discuss world events but I was aware of the prisoners' news embargo, mainly insisted upon by the Russians. Therefore, what follows is neither a biography of Speer, nor a pre-empting of his subsequent biographers who, after all, interviewed him after his release; by then he was a man damaged from the rigours of twenty difficult years in prison.

His subsequent biographers saw him in a different light. He was famous, now a free man, albeit a man who needed an income, and they paid him handsomely for his highly marketable accounts. Speer knew full well what the public wanted to hear, and he took every opportunity, via television, radio, newspapers and journals, to explain the unexplainable – how he had lived the luxurious life of a close confidant to Hitler through all the horrors of Nazism, yet remained especially ignorant of the plight of Jews and concentration camp prisoners, in camps he designed. By manipulating his post-prison autobiographies and interviews, Speer successfully created, then improved upon, the image of a man who, although a senior Nazi minister, had managed to remain ignorant of the horrific criminal brutality towards civilians and mass destruction of some of Europe's finest cities all ordered by the Nazi leaders, and Speer held a senior position in their very midst. His daughter, Margret, wrote in her 2005 memoirs that after his release from Spandau he spent all of his time consolidating the lucrative 'Speer Myth'.[2]

This image of his relative innocence had earlier formed the basis of his defence at the 1946 Nuremberg trials, giving rise to the suspicion that Speer had longed planned the 'not me' defence by claiming he was a 'decent fellow in the wrong place'. When challenged in court for his various departments using concentration camp prisoners, he put all the blame for any mistreatment on to the shoulders of his deputy, Fritz Sauckel, who unwittingly played along with the concept by antagonising the judges with his arrogance and pomposity, for which he went to the gallows at the conclusion of his trial. Speer's alleged innocence and plea that while he knew little of all these 'dreadful things', his only guilt related to him not enquiring what was happening. He was also shrewd enough to be the only defendant to admit his part in the accused's collective guilt for the war, just by being there as opposed to having had any part in, or personal knowledge of all the horrors of Nazism. He also found favour with the judges by having fully cooperated with the Allies following his arrest, and claiming that he alone had stood against Hitler by countermanding Hitler's final order to destroy Germany's infrastructure during the final days of the war. Speer's respectful demeanour to the judges and his 'not culpable' position was sufficient for his account to be accepted by the judges; although he made a curious comment in his later book, *Spandau: The Secret Diaries* when he wrote of the trial: 'So lies, smokescreens, and dissembling statements have paid off after all.'

His duplicity certainly saved his neck. It was an approach and image he continued to expertly craft and polish in the years following his release from prison. He was desperate to be seen as the 'clean German', willing to divert responsibility for German war crimes away from the surviving German people, and on to those senior Nazis found guilty at Nuremberg. Following his release from prison, this hypothesis led to the suspicion that Speer was deliberately providing Germans with evidence that not all of them were guilty of war crimes. He sought to create an acceptable alibi for a whole new generation of Germans, all desperately seeking collective forgiveness from the rest of the world.

It may, therefore, help the reader to know a little of Speer's upbringing, and a brief outline should suffice to explain some of the pressures experienced by this complicated young man, pressures which, in his twenties, encouraged him to ally himself to Hitler. Throughout his pre-prison life, Speer never lacked for money or privilege. His grandfather had been a prosperous architect in Dortmund, but died at an early age leaving four sons, one of whom followed suit and became a well-known architect in Mannheim and lived very comfortably, marrying a wealthy lady. They had three sons, with Albert between older brother Hermann and younger brother Ernst. The Speers were highly conventional, verging on the ostentatious; they were traditional pillars of German high society living in a most prestigious house with a gated courtyard. Their furniture was the most elegant money could buy. While growing up, Speer and his brothers enjoyed the services of a French governess, who ensured they were always correctly dressed and on time for meals, family occasions and school. The house was run by a full-time staff of uniformed servants and cooks, which included a uniformed chauffeur to drive their two Mercedes cars. Private cars were rare, no other Mannheim family owned two cars, one of which was always parked outside the Speer house as an obvious display of their elevated standing in the community. Although the children's education was private, Speer remembered being fascinated by stories and photographs of the First World War. War would have still been in the background of German life, even for a wealthy family, who also had to survive on whatever food their wealth could buy, especially when little food was available. It was a period when turnips were a staple diet for everyone.

Albert was regularly bullied by Hermann, which resulted in him becoming progressively withdrawn. He loved sport and mountain climbing, but such activities were viewed by his parents as proletarian; this background may have nudged him towards being a loner, albeit a highly intelligent and confident loner. As a 17-year-old walking home from school, he met his future wife, Margarete, a girl from an 'ordinary' background who was never accepted or made welcome at the Speer home.

Albert was always the star pupil at school, especially as he possessed an unusual understanding and love of complex mathematics. He completed his studies with high accolade, but strong parental pressure forced him towards a career in architecture. From 1923 he attended university at Karlsruhe with the intention of following his father into architecture. He found Karlsruhe 'boring', and in 1924 he transferred to Munich University. He received a moderate monthly allowance, in US dollars, following a family sale of a business concluded in that currency, which made his life as a student easy. Speer was, therefore, immune from the suffering of millions of impoverished Germans during the period of high inflation that swept Germany, and he delighted in holding weekly spaghetti meatball suppers at his student flat for his hungry student friends.

In 1927, the 23-year-old Speer completed his architectural studies. Now well-qualified, he continued at the university as a salaried tutor, which enabled him to marry Margarete before seeking work through his father's business. The wedding ceremony took place in Berlin without his parents who, he maintained, declined to attend. Speer once said that, on reflection, he possibly didn't invite them; they refused to meet the new Frau Speer during the first seven years of their married life.

Like many young Germans, Speer supported the collective belief that the Allied Versailles Treaty was responsible for starving the German people, and he joined the Nazi Party in 1931, after having attended a Hitler rally for students. Speer had been encouraged to attend the rally with a group of his own students, and found the experience mesmerising. He described the experience in glowing terms:

I was carried away on the wave of the enthusiasm which, one could almost feel this physically, bore the speaker along from sentence to sentence. It swept away any scepticism, any reservations. Opponents were given no chance to speak. This furthered the illusion, at least momentarily, of unanimity. Finally, Hitler no longer seemed to be speaking to convince; rather he seemed to feel that he was expressing what the audience, by now transformed into a single mass, expected of him.

He added:

> It was an utterly undramatic decision. Then and ever afterward I scarcely felt myself to be a member of a political party. I was not choosing the NSDAP, but becoming a follower of Hitler, whose magnetic force had reached out to me the first time I saw him and had not, hereafter, released me... I knew nothing about his program. He had taken hold of me before I grasped what was happening.[3]

The following day he joined the Nazi Party, but like most young Germans he joined to be 'one of the crowd', not bothering to enquire about the basis or aspirations of the party. He ignored his usually sharp critical awareness for the benefits he thought he could achieve. Nevertheless, from his first casual meeting with the fledgling Nazi Party, until the end of the Second World War, Speer remained a civilian and later claimed never to have been a 'real' Nazi.

Albert Speer's early and rapid progression was extraordinary. From being a freshly qualified but out-of-work architect aged just 23, his architectural career received impetus when, four weeks after the Reichstag fire, he was urgently summoned to go to Berlin. Someone called 'Goebbels', the *Gauleiter* of Berlin, the city's senior official, had seen photographs of one of Speer's projects and wanted to meet him. Although an impoverished architect in a land of mass unemployment, Speer unexpectedly obtained the contract to help supervise the construction of the new district headquarters. Speer's temporary office was in the centre of the government district, next to President Hindenburg's office, he could readily observe the president and his entourage walking between various government departments. Success followed success for Speer, who soon heard his style of work was quietly being admired by Hitler, a former amateur landscape artist and equally keen amateur architect. The date 11 March 1933 was an unforgettable day for Speer; he accompanied Goebbels, the newly appointed Nazi minister of Propaganda, to his offices on Wilhelmplatz, the smartest location in Berlin. Goebbels wanted his imposing new office suite to be completely redecorated to his personal specifications. Speer confirmed everything was possible, so Goebbels commissioned him on the spot. The work was completed in just two weeks; Speer's teams worked non-stop, with Speer supervising much of the night work. Goebbels was delighted with the result and gave the young architect his next project: to design the special effects for the forthcoming

Nazi rally at Berlin's Templehof Airport. The result was an impressive light show, which impressed Hitler – although the success was claimed by Goebbels.

Now people in high places realised they had someone in their midst with a special talent. Hitler's deputy, Rudolf Hess, summoned Speer to Nuremberg to oversee preparations for the forthcoming Nazi rally and May Day celebrations. Speer produced his plans, which impressed Hess, only to be told 'only the Führer can decide, he is in his office, go and see him now'. As Speer cautiously entered the Führer's office, Hitler was examining a pistol. Hitler put the pistol down and laid out Speer's plans on a table, 'Agreed,' was all that Hitler said and resumed examining the firearm. This pistol was Hitler's personal weapon, and it was with this weapon that his first lover, his niece Geli Raubal, had allegedly committed suicide.

Three months later Speer was appointed to assist the renowned German architect, Professor Paul Troost, to rebuild the Reich Chancellor's (Hitler's) personal apartments in Berlin. Hitler took a keen interest as the work progressed and towards the end of one particular visit, he approached the young Speer and invited him to lunch. Bemused, Speer followed Hitler into the exclusive dining room where the day's lunch guests were already gathering. Speer realised he still had plaster dust on his jacket and Hitler noticed the young man's embarrassment. Hitler took Speer directly to his private apartment and instructed his valet to find a suitable jacket. Now wearing Hitler's jacket, complete with the Führer insignia, the two returned to join the other guests, where Speer was introduced by Hitler. Most guests knew the significance of the Führer jacket, complete with its discreet gold swastika. Goebbels could not resist openly asking about the jacket. Hitler responded by ignoring Goebbels and inviting the 28-year-old Speer to sit next to him, the most powerful man in Germany, for lunch. Hitler had a real skill in making those around him feel protected, or isolated, from external events. From 1933 this favour would extend to Speer.

Within weeks, Speer was appointed as Hitler's architect before being promoted to become the General Inspector of Buildings for the new Reich Capital of Berlin; this involved designing *Germania*, the new world capital. Speer was quick to establish his own business with himself as senior consultant; large consultancy fees soon found their way into Speer's accounts, to which was added huge profits from the sale of land, conveniently acquired by Speer in advance of *Germania* being announced. Later, at the Nuremberg trials, it was unbeknown, or overlooked by the judges, that Speer had authorised the eviction and deportation of Berlin's property-rich Jewish community, who owned much of the land required for the project. He also commandeered several hundred of the finest Jewish properties in central Berlin, which Speer used as favours or gifts for prominent party members. Speer is alleged to have rather flippantly commented, 'in recent times a number of Jews fled Germany leaving their debts behind them'.[4] Other top Nazis were more blatant: Neurath, the country's Foreign Minister, simply had a Jewish industrialist evicted from his fine country house and estate, while Ribbentrop committed the owner of another Berlin estate and properties in Austria to a concentration camp to be murdered, but only after the estates had been 'signed over' to Ribbentrop. While Jews were in the process of being evicted, Berlin's Chief of Police, Count Helldorf, devised and operated a hugely profitable scheme whereby rich evicted Jews could obtain exit visas from the police. Helldorf simply ordered the confiscation of their passports but then gave the owners the right to purchase them back, stamped with the exit visa. The cost of each redemption, in modern terms, would have been £25,000. Helldorf later made the biggest mistake of his life when, just a few days prior to the plot to kill Hitler, and without really knowing what was being plotted, he intimated that he would 'hold back' the Berlin police to maintain order across the city. Unfortunately for Helldorf, his intimation to 'hold back' was recorded by the plotters and when that information fell into the hands of the Gestapo, he was immediately arrested. Following the usual interrogation he was, specifically on Hitler's orders, forced to watch his fellow conspirators being hanged before his own execution.[5]

However, unlike other Nazi leaders, neither Hitler nor Speer openly engaged in amassing plunder from Europe's museums or bank vaults. Disliking Goering's lust for stolen property, and the Nazi system of paying or extorting bribes and expensive 'gifts' from contractors or well-off draft dodgers, Speer issued an order to his officials to the effect that they were not to accept expensive gifts to smooth the awarding of contracts. He stated that he could not 'protect any collaborators who contravene this order'.[6] The matter of Speer's collection of stolen paintings will be dealt with shortly.

Speer's power base relied totally on his relationship with Hitler, who described him as well-mannered and confident. Speer's ability included his skill at thwarting any ambitious or talented underlings by appointing them to suitable and demanding positions elsewhere. His open and unlimited access to Hitler gave him power above other ministers, such as Himmler and Goering. If Hitler agreed with Speer, then the decision automatically became Hitler's. In order to be close to Hitler at his Obersalzberg mountain retreat, Speer acquired a comfortable house with a studio within walking distance of Hitler's Berghof.

In 1943 Speer became Minister of Armaments and War Production, which gave him both massive power and responsibility for armaments production, transportation and placement, along with the final authority over raw materials and industrial production. During this time production in Germany peaked, and Speer proved to be an essential factor that boosted Germany's fighting abilities by mobilizing German's industry, although conscription and slave labour from concentration camps was extensively used. Speer admitted at Nuremberg that 40 per cent of all prisoners of war were employed in the production of weapons and munitions, and in subsidiary industries. Speer also sought to draft women into war production industries as happened in the UK, where two and a quarter million women were so employed, but Hitler refused and retaliated by ordering the drafting into the army of many of Speer's skilled workers, thus seriously reducing war production.[7]

Speer was certainly a hard worker, and a demanding task master. He required perfect paperwork and meticulous craftsmanship. His attention to detail was to inadvertently save many lives. Speer ordered that, to protect German munitions workers and military personnel, all heavy shells and bombs were to be embossed with a code specifying exactly what the bomb contained, and, most importantly, a code indicating any enclosed booby trap. With German efficiency, these code details were officially recorded under German patent laws, details of which came the Allies way during the war. A post-war senior British Army bomb disposal officer once commented that Speer had made the disposal of unexploded German munitions and bombs more straightforward, as bomb disposal teams knew exactly what they were dealing with.[8]

In January 1944, Speer became ill with an infection in his knee, and on Hitler's advice, was treated for three months at the Hohenlychen clinic just north of Berlin. The clinic was run by SS Dr Gebhardt, infamous for experimental surgery on prisoners. Speer was fully aware that a number of highly placed Nazi officials, who had earned the displeasure of the top echelon, had mysteriously died at Hohenlychen. Speer was deeply suspicious of Gebhardt, who began treating him for a heart complaint – which he did not have, and thought the doctor might be under instruction to murder him. Fortunately for Speer, his secretary, Fraulein Kempf, had remained at his side as Speer insisted on being kept informed of his ministry's progress. When Speer suddenly, and for no obvious reason, became seriously ill, she called Margarete, his wife, who was sufficiently concerned and took another doctor with her, one that she could trust, Professor Friedrich Koch. He found Speer heavily drugged with Dr Gebhardt preparing to operate on Speer's lungs. Dr Koch stopped the operation and, without further medication, Speer immediately began to recover. By the following day he had no untoward physical symptoms. Understandably, Speer believed that Dr Gebhardt was going to kill him.[9]

Speer needed to recuperate from his illness, and with summer coming, and to escape Dr Gebhardt, he and his wife moved to Castle Klessheim in Austria, the German Foreign Office's lavish guest facility near Salzburg. He was there for two months before he was reunited with Hitler. Speer found Hitler indifferent and it was from this point that Speer became disillusioned with him. From Salzburg, the Speers went on a six-week holiday to Castel Goyen near Merano, Italy. Aware that Hitler's coterie had been ganging up against him during his illness, and because he was being 'protected' by teams of SS bodyguards, even while on holiday, he decided to bring matters into the open and resigned as Minister of Armaments and War Production. For effect, the resignation letter reached Hitler just in time for his birthday; Hitler was not amused.

A long-standing friend of Speer, the industrialist Walter 'Panzer' Rohland, was sent from Hitler's birthday party at the Berghof to plead with Speer to reconsider matters. Rohland informed Speer that, with the war now lost, it was his opinion that Hitler would destroy Germany and only Speer could thwart him. Speer agreed to reconsider his position. Speer then flew to see Hitler at the Berghof where he was greeted by a reasonably friendly Hitler; Speer's resignation was formally withdrawn and Speer cautiously returned to work.

By the end of 1944, and with the German military losing their battles, Speer realised the defeat of Germany was inevitable; he nevertheless continued to promote industry and dubiously claimed he was still increasing production. Under Speer's direction, Germany's economic and armaments production reached its wartime peak, despite being subjected to heavy Allied bombing, but only 7 per cent of their machinery was ever completely destroyed. This high level of economic production was largely possible by using some 5 million forced labour and concentration camp prisoners; many were working in Speer's underground factories. One such underground establishment was at Mittelbau-Dora, hidden away to the south of Hannover in the picturesque Harz Mountains. The huge complex was built and quickly brought to full production following the successful Allied bombing of Peenemunde, the V2 rocket factory located on an offshore Baltic island in northern Germany. These underground factories were death traps for workers forced to live underground in appalling conditions; discipline was brutal, with regular executions. There was no first aid; those who were too weak or awkward went to the 'sanatorium'.

As was typical for concentration camp prisoners, they were indistinguishable having to wear a rough uniform with a striped pattern which would not get washed, so were covered in lice, which spread typhus among the prisoners. There were so many corpses at underground Dora, that the crematorium was frequently overwhelmed. Speer's own staff described the conditions there as 'hell'.[10]

By 13 February 1945, the Allies were approaching Berlin from all sides. Hitler ordered that Germany was to be left as one vast 'wasteland'. Army generals, district *Gauleiters* and Reich defence commissioners were charged with carrying out the order. Bridges, dams, factories, farms, military and civilian supply lines, power stations and rail lines were all to be blown up or otherwise destroyed. If followed, the order would have seen Germany reduced to a pre-industrial agricultural economy, with the surviving population suffering widespread starvation, poverty and disease. A common expression then heard across Germany was 'Everything is shit, but we've still got the Führer'.[11] The official order was named *Destructive Measures on Reich Territory*, but was nicknamed the *Nero Decree*, after the Roman emperor who 'fiddled' as he watched Rome burn during the great fire of AD 64.

Speer now realised that, with Germany facing defeat and Hitler's ministers all but powerless, he assumed the position of being Hitler's number two, the second most powerful man in Germany. This realisation gave Speer the authority and power to turn against Hitler's policy, which was aimed as much at destroying the German people as it was to slowing the Allied advance across Germany itself. Speer knew the German people were especially anxious about what lay in store for them when overrun by the Russian advance; the prospect of revenge was terrifying them after their own earlier brutal treatment of the Russians. The *Wehrmacht* had taken the lives of 23 million Soviet citizens, roughly half of them civilians so that when the tide of the war finally turned, vengeful Russian forces poured into Germany and their inexorable advance became an orgy of uncontrolled destruction, plunder, rape and murder. But Hitler was not concerned by the prospect, he had come to believe the German people had abandoned him, so sought to drag the entire country with him into the looming inferno. Speer objected in a typically outspoken memorandum:

> We have no right at this stage of the war to carry out demolitions which might affect the life of the people. If our enemies wish to destroy this nation, which has fought with unique bravery, then this historical shame shall rest exclusively upon them.

Hitler ignored Speer and authorised his 'scorched earth' order to commence. Speer nevertheless initiated his own plan to interrupt Hitler's orders, and with the support of a number of influential generals, ameliorated the action and saved much of the German infrastructure. At his trial he also claimed to have planned to murder Hitler by poisoning him through the conference bunker's air-conditioning while Hitler was ensconced with his close advisers. There is no evidence that this was true but Speer later claimed that in February 1944 he had asked Dieter Stahl, head of chemical research, for poison gas with which to murder Hitler, but then abandoned the plan due to technical difficulties. Although the supply of gas was confirmed, the air intake ducts intended by Speer to introduce the gas had been raised from ground level to 10 feet above ground, making the ducts inaccessible. This 'assassination' information only came to light during Speer's trial, and doubts remain about his intention to actually carry out the plan; many believe it was a fantasy to soften the Nuremberg judges at his trial. They asked, how was it that the Minister of Armaments was unable to find a short ladder?[12] Even so, by countermanding Hitler's direct orders, Speer had placed himself, and those around him, in grave danger; Speer knew this.

Speer also claimed to me that during his trial he had sent a secret memorandum to the trial judges stating that he had offered to mobilise the surviving German army to link with the advancing Western Allies in order to drive the invading Russians back to Russia, and thereby save Eastern Europe from Communism. His memo was not acknowledged. However, and coincidently, at the end of the war Churchill had requested an investigation into the feasibility of the Allies cooperating with the remains of the German Army; the plan under consideration was to attack Russia once Germany surrendered. The operation was named 'Operation Unthinkable' but was vetoed by the Allied commanders.

By April 1945, little was left of Speer's armaments industry and he had few official duties. On 20 April Speer flew to the *Führerbunker* in Berlin where he met with Hitler and toured the damaged chancellery, which Speer had originally designed, before celebrating Hitler's 56th birthday. The next day he drove to Hamburg to join the new but self-appointed national cabinet of ministers being formed under Admiral Dönitz. At that time Speer's staff described him as 'depressed'.

On 23 April, Speer horrified his personal staff by returning to Berlin, allegedly to see Hitler for the last time. He was flown in a training aircraft from Mecklenburg to Gatow on the outskirts of Berlin, where he switched to a Fiesler Fi 156 Storch, an aircraft capable of a short take-off and landing such as on a football field or short stretch of road.[13] Escorted by a fighter plane, the Storch pilot somehow managed to land in near darkness on the bomb-cratered track across the Tiergarten, the wide open park between the Victory Column and the Brandenburg Gate. Speer commandeered a passing army truck and was taken to the chancellery, where he was led down several flights of concrete steps to Hitler's bunker. In a disjointed and lengthy conversation with Hitler, Speer confessed to Hitler that his public conscience would force him to disobey the scorched-earth policy. Hitler hardly responded and went to his bedroom leaving Speer with Goebbels, who told Speer that he and the Goebbels family would die with Hitler. In an atmosphere described by Speer as 'unreal', Speer escaped the descending lunacy infecting those still in the bunker by spending the last few hours of Eva's life, ' between midnight and three in the morning, with her drinking *Moet et Chandon* champagne and nibbling cakes in her small bedroom'.[14]

Speer then went to Hitler's private room where he was virtually ignored by him, except for a 'So, you are leaving – auf wiedersehen.' With Eva still refusing to leave, it was back to the waiting Storch amidst exploding Russian shells. En route back to Hamburg, Speer was flown to the hospital north of Berlin, where he had recovered from his earlier illness, to see Himmler, who was planning to assist the Allies by offering to be their national chief of police. Speer then flew back to Hamburg to join Dönitz's 'alternative' government at nearby Flensburg where he did what he could to save Germany's network of bridges, factories and other installations vital to the country's survival. Just six days later, on 29 April, the day before committing suicide, Hitler dropped Speer from the successor government. Speer was disappointed that Hitler had not selected him as his successor.

After Hitler's death, Hitler's faithful and longtime valet, Julius Schaub, went straight to the Berghof with Hitler's personal safe keys. On arrival there he emptied the various safes and made a large fire on the Berghof veranda of Hitler's and Eva Braun's personal documents. Without much doubt, these papers would have been of great interest to the Allies and historians alike. Speer immediately offered his services to the so-called Flensburg Government of post-war Germany, meeting daily at Glücksburg Castle and headed by Hitler's appointed successor, Karl Dönitz. Speer took a meaningless role in that short-lived and powerless regime as Minister of Industry and Production. No doubt anxious for his future, Speer willingly forwarded information to the Allies regarding the effects of the air war, and on a broad range of subjects, beginning on 10 May. A few days later, American military specialists arrived, led by Paul Nitze of the United States Strategic Bombing Survey, along with a team of interpreters and assistants. They were curious to learn from Speer how German industry had survived so well in spite of constant US and RAF bombing. They questioned Speer for ten successive days, during which he talked freely taking them through what he termed as 'bombing high school'. Each morning Speer would politely answer their questions; being aware he was touchy about war crimes, and because they were primarily concerned with the success or otherwise of USA bombing policy, they avoided the subject. Speer cleverly played on his indispensability to the Americans and worked on the 'Speer spell'. One senior American commented, 'he evoked in us a sympathy of which we were all secretly ashamed'.[15]

On 23 May, two weeks after the surrender of German forces, British troops arrived at Glücksburg Castle to arrest Speer, along with other members of the Flensburg Government. This brought Nazi Germany to a formal end, and the beginning of the Nuremberg War Crimes trials. With the arrest of the Flensburg Government, the German High Command also ceased to exist.

Chapter Three

Understanding Albert Speer 1905–1945: His Personal Timeline

Albert Speer was born in Mannheim on 19 March 1905 into an affluent upper-class family. He was the second of three sons of Luise Máthilde Wilhelmine (Hommel) and Albert Friedrich Speer. In 1918 the family leased their Mannheim residence and moved to another of their properties in Heidelberg. His brothers, Ernst and Hermann, bullied him throughout his childhood. Speer was active in sports, taking up skiing and mountaineering. He was clever in class and invariably top in all mathematics examinations; maths was his favourite subject. Due to parental pressure, he was obliged to abandon his love of mathematics at university to follow his father and grandfather into architecture, where he could earn a respectable income.

Albert Speer Timeline

1923: Speer attended the University of Karlsruhe.

1924: He transferred to the 'much more reputable' Technical University of Munich.

1925: He transferred again, this time to the Technical University of Berlin where he studied under the famous Heinrich Tessenow, whom Speer greatly admired.

1927: Passing his exams, and aged only 22, Speer became Professor Tessenow's assistant and taught some of Tessenow's classes, while continuing his own postgraduate studies.

Since Munich, Speer had nurtured a close friendship with a fellow student, Rudolf Wolters, who also studied under Tessenow. It was a friendship that ultimately spanned more than 50 years.

1928:   On 28 August, Albert Speer secretly married Margarete (Margret) Weber in Berlin. Speer had begun courting Margarete while she was still at school; she was the daughter of a successful craftsman who employed fifty workers. Their relationship was frowned upon by Speer's upper-class-conscious mother, who felt the Webers were socially inferior. It was several years before the two Speer families united, although the relationship between the two women remained taut.

1930:   Speer first heard Hitler speak at a beer hall in Berlin. Speer was impressed with the leader, and by Speer's senior professors, who had been specially invited guests, and were also in awe of Hitler. Mesmerised by the impact of the event, and Hitler's oratory, Speer joined the NSDAP, later known as the Nazi Party. His membership number was 474,481.

1932:   As an automobile owner, Speer was hired to drive Hitler around Berlin.

1933:   Speer was offered lucrative work by Goebbels and moved to Berlin to design his client's new office. During the same year, Speer created the 'Cathedral of Lights' for the May Day rally at Berlin's Templehof Airport. Hitler was impressed by Speer's work, recognising it as that of a very talented architect; this resulted in Speer being chosen to supervise the redesign of Hitler's residence in Berlin. It was after a successful inspection by Hitler of the work in progress, that Speer was invited by the Führer to attend the day's lunch party. It was the first step for Speer to move into Hitler's inner circle, and he soon became Hitler's personal architect. Because they both shared the same interest for architecture, Speer became one of Hitler's confidants. Although his office in Berlin was in sight of the Reichstag, Speer maintained he knew nothing about the Reichstag fire.

1934:   Hitler's architect, Paul Troost, and the Reich President Hindenburg, both died. Speer was rewarded with his first of many important commissions: the design of the huge parade grounds, searchlights, and banners for the spectacular Nuremberg Rally, which was such an enormous success that it was filmed by Leni Riefenstahl and titled

Triumph of the Will. Speer commented, 'I felt myself to be Hitler's architect. Political events did not concern me. My job was merely to provide impressive backdrops for such events.'

It was also the year of the momentous Röhm *putsch*; to me, Speer maintained he knew nothing about Röhm, the leader of the notorious Nazi Brownshirts, or the *putsch* to unseat Röhm. It was an infamous and widely publicized action, and acclaimed across Germany as necessary for Hitler to save Germany from an imminent coup. In the free world the press were under no such illusion; they estimated the arrests at over 500. Later, in 1970, Speer wrote of the *putsch* in his *Inside the Third Reich*

> I was in Berlin during the Röhm *putsch* (June) and tension hung in the city. Soldiers in battle array were encamped in the Tiergarten [park adjacent to the Brandenburg Gate]. Trucks full of police holding rifles cruised the streets. There was clearly an air of something cooking.

This comment suggests that Speer was already practising the art of claiming how little he knew of important, dramatic, or well-publicized national events outside his official circle.

1935:   Speer disposed of his less prestigious house in Berlin to 'acquire' a fine lakeside house on the Wannsee, a property formally owned by a Jewish film star. A number of other prestigious lakeside properties were similarly signed over to Speer. He then acquired a fine mountainside home near Hitler's Berghof in the Obersalzberg. This elegant property had, unsurprisingly, previously been owned by a wealthy Jewish family, who had been advised to emigrate. With homes now established in both Berlin and the Obersalzberg, Speer had effectively made himself accessible to be at Hitler's beck and call.

1936:   Speer designed the German pavilion for the World Fair held in Paris in 1937.

1937:   Speer was appointed to the position of Inspector General of Construction for the Reich Capital, becoming a senior public servant, answerable only to Hitler. During the year, he was assigned to design and build the new Reich Chancellery. In the same year, Speer moved his family to Obersaltberg, the private alpine retreat in which Hitler and members of his inner circle lived. He visited Hitler once or twice a week for dinner, and increasingly deserted his family to be of service to Hitler, and to provide discreet company for Hitler's lady friend and possible mistress, Eva Braun. Eva had first met the 40-year-old Hitler as a 17-year-old trainee while she was working for his official photographer. After wooing the girl at a number of discreet restaurants, Eva secretly moved in with Hitler. Over the following years, especially at the Berghof, Hitler's inevitable late night briefings with his generals meant that Eva spent long hours alone with Speer, who, being a civilian, never attended the regular late night military briefings. Eva Braun was one of the most successfully guarded secrets of Nazi Germany; she was kept at the Berghof in semi-concealment and entered the lair by side entrances, or its rear staircase. Access to her family and friends was severely restricted and supervised by Hitler's SS bodyguards; however, Eva Braun held a strong position within the hierarchy of Hitler's inner circle. To be invited to the Berghof it was absolutely necessary to get on well with Eva; her main hobby was photography and she sold a number of her private pictures of Hitler to Heinrich Hoffmann, earning a lot of money in the process. A number of the photographs published by Hoffmann in his famous picture books about the life of Hitler were taken by Eva Braun. Her diaries were destroyed at the end of the war by Hitler's valet.

1938:   Speer was awarded the Nazi Party's Gold Badge of Honour. He continued to design for Hitler up until 1942 and was then given the task of redesigning the city of Berlin, to be known as *Germania*, the finest and most important city in all of Europe. Hitler's wish was for the project to be completed in the early 1950s, but work was halted by the war. Speer was now a millionaire.

To commence the construction of *Germania*, Speer's contractors needed massive stockpiles of land, and stone from some 200 quarries; they used prisoners of war and slave labour at the early stages of construction. Much of Berlin's land and residential area, over 25,000 homes, was Jewish owned; these were confiscated by

Speer's department, rendering large numbers of Jews homeless. These unfortunate people were evicted, then rounded up, and passed to the SS and Gestapo for transport to various extermination camps. Speer enlisted the assistance of Reinhard Heydrich, Deputy Director of Bohemia and Moravia, to provide slave labour for the project. Heydrich provided some 15,000 Czech prisoners in exchange for Speer redesigning Prague to his grandiose plans. Speer claimed to me that he had never met or heard of Heydrich.

1939: War production and housing for his large workforce began to hinder Speer's grandiose construction work across Berlin. Having obtained the legal right to Jewish property, Speer resolved the housing issue by progressively evicting Jews from their properties. After *Kristallnacht*, the flow of Jewish refugees from Berlin averaged 3,000 per month. Speer gained valuable favours by using the more prestigious properties as gifts given to a number of officials on Heydrich's staff, Goebbels' and Himmler's friends, and to senior army officers.

1941: All Jewish emigration from the Reich was prohibited. With thousands of Berliners rendered homeless by bombing, Speer and Goebbels agreed that Adolf Eichmann should commence the expulsion of all Jews from Berlin; he was already in the process of such action in Austria. The expulsions commenced in August, and by the end of the month, the problem of evicted, and in consequence, homeless Jews, was resolved by rounding them up and transporting them to extermination camps. Detailed extermination statistics were promulgated to all ministries and agencies, including those under Speer's control.

With over 5 million German workers drafted into the German military to replace those killed or wounded, Speer replaced them with Russian prisoners of war. Being under the control of the SS, conditions for such prisoners were grim. Speer understood workers needed food; conversely, the SS saw work as an extension of their 'extermination by work' policy. Such worker replacement was shortly to include concentration camp inmates deemed fit enough, in the short term, to work. When Speer complained to Hitler about the difficulty of maintaining his vast workforce, Hitler agreed to allow Speer to use concentration camp inmates in a number of industries that were short of manpower, including Professor Porsche's vehicle manufacturing industry.

1942:   Aged 37, Speer was appointed Minister for Armaments and Munitions, succeeding the engineer, Doctor Fritz Todt. Speer's younger brother, Ernst, was killed at Stalingrad.

Speer founded the 'Baustab Speer-Ostbau' (Speer construction East) to undertake heavy construction in the East and Ukraine, including the construction of a motorway linking Germany with Ukraine. Known as the SS Road, it used concentration camp inmates, mainly Jews, who were supplied by the SS on a plan authorised by Himmler under the heading 'Annihilation Through Work'. When Jewish workers collapsed, or were unwell, they were executed; the SS recorded nearly ninety such mass executions during the project.[1] Some 50,000 extra workers were supplied by the *Wehrmacht* (German Army).

Speer also used Russian prisoners of war to help clear bomb damage across Berlin. Conditions were equally fierce for these unfortunates, and economic measures precluded feeding them at weekends.

By the year's end, Speer's staff had surrendered over 7,000 Jewish families to the Gestapo for transportation to extermination camps. Jews were now officially deemed to be 'enemies of the state'.

1943:   Speer's factories were desperately short of manpower, so Speer obtained Hitler's permission to recruit 'volunteer' French workers. By pressurizing the French Vichy government, an order was made to require all French males aged 18 to 55, and childless females from 21 to 35, to be conscripted for such work in Germany. Due to conditions, few regularly reported for work, with many disappearing into the French countryside instead of reporting for work. Speer neatly solved the problem by converting French factories to the German war effort, enabling the workers to stay in France.

1944:   On 30 January, Speer drew up a memorandum for Hitler titled 'The war is lost', and gave numerous reasons why. Speer then worked against Hitler's scorched-earth policy, known as 'Operation Nero', which aimed to destroy German infrastructure in order to hinder Allied reconstruction. Germany's economic and armaments production reached its wartime peak despite being under heavy Allied bombing. By now, Speer realised that the war was inevitably lost, but he continued to promote industry, and to maintain production. Kitchen said: 'There can be no doubt that Speer did indeed help to prolong the war longer than many thought possible, as a result of which, further millions were killed and Germany reduced to a pile of rubble.'[2]

Speer claimed he decided to murder Hitler; his plan was to poison him through the air-conditioning, but later changed his mind. While this claim remains doubtful, he certainly did what he could to save the country's factories and other installations, all vital to the post-war survival of Germany. With regard to bridges, in Berlin just 80 bridges were destroyed out of nearly 1,000 ordered by Hitler for destruction. The date 20 July saw the failed plot by Count von Stauffenberg to kill Hitler. Speer is alleged to have been in some contact with the plotters, though there is no evidence suggesting his knowledge or participation. Even so, Speer was on the plotters list to be their Minister of Armaments in the prospective post-coup government. Following the plotters' arrests, unsurprisingly, Speer condemned the plotters. He was asked about his name on the list as a potential minister but he was able to convince his questioners that he was unaware of the plot. He would have realised the precariousness of his position at the time.[3]

Following the plot, Speer came under some suspicion, but his remaining strong link to Hitler was maintained due to Hitler believing in Speer's involvement with the V-rocket programmes. By the end of the year, Speer had some 200,000 Mittelbau-Dora concentration camp inmates working on his missile project; due to conditions, half died. When he visited the project, his accompanying staff officers were shocked by the conditions. Speer ambiguously commented in his memoirs (*Erinnerungen*) 'the sight of people suffering affected my feelings but not my actions'. When the Americans liberated Mittelbau-Dora they found identically unbelievable conditions; there were thousands of bodies stacked in piles, some had been shot, while others had died from brutality or starvation. In the final analysis, the missile projects, made infamous by the V1 and V2 programmes, were largely inconsequential when compared with the more successful Luftwaffe bombing.

Realising that Germany faced Armageddon, at least from the Russians, one of Speer's last reports concluded with the words, 'May God protect Germany.'

1945: On 23 May, Albert Speer was among the twenty-four major war criminals arrested by the British at Flensburg in northern Germany. The prisoners were transferred to the Palace Hotel in Luxembourg, then to Versailles near Paris, before being sent on to Kransberg Castle in the German state of Hesse, which Speer had once renovated. Their final holding point was at Nuremberg which they reached on 10 August. To his surprise and disappointment, Speer was charged with war crimes and ordered to appear at the special trial for the top Nazi leaders.

1946: Speer was convicted of two war crimes against humanity and sentenced to serve twenty years' imprisonment in Spandau Prison in West Berlin.

1966: Released from Spandau Prison.

Timeline of principal events, well-known to German nationals, and by implication as a senior Nazi minister, by Reich Minister Albert Speer

1933: From 1 April
The public burning of books written by Jews and those deemed by the authorities to be anti-Nazis. Personal attacks by German civilians against the Jews and their property are state encouraged. All police and legal regulations and laws to protect Jews are abolished. Germans are ordered to boycott all shops and businesses owned by Jews. By force of numbers, the SA picketed these shops to prevent people entering. The Jewish ritual slaughter of animals is banned. The legal 'Department of Racial Hygiene' better known as 'ethnic cleansing' is established.

Nazis compile statistics on the 'Rhineland Bastards'. The Prussian minister of the interior, Hermann Goering, asks local authorities to provide statistics concerning this group, specifically targeting black Germans who were the offspring of German women and French colonial soldiers who served in the French occupation force in

Germany in the 1920s. Also affected were the children of German colonialists, who married African women and returned with them to Germany in the aftermath of the First World War. Demands were made to end the 'black curse' by sterilisation of all mixed-race people. Doctors instructed to target Romani people for sterilisation.

1934: Jewish students excluded from exams in medicine, dentistry, pharmacy and law. Male Jews were legally excluded from military service.

1935: New Nuremberg Laws were enacted; these were anti-Semitic and racist and denied Jews many basic civil rights. A law for 'The Protection of German Blood and German Honour' forbade mixed marriages.

1936: • Jews were no longer allowed to vote and lost German citizenship.
   • Benefit payments to Jewish families stopped.
   • Jews banned from parks, restaurants and swimming pools.
   • Jews forbidden to use the German greeting 'Heil Hitler'.
   • Jews no longer allowed ownership of electrical/optical equipment, bicycles, typewriters or records.
   • Passports for Jews to travel abroad restricted.
   • Many Jewish students removed from German schools and universities.

Within the framework of open Nazi antagonism towards the Jewish population, eminent and famous Jews who had not fled Germany were publicly rounded up to join the ongoing mass deportations of Jews for extermination, many to Riga in Latvia. Typical was Lilli Henhoch, the popular German national and world record holder in multiple sports. Being Jewish, she was refused the opportunity of representing Germany at the 1936 Berlin Olympic Games, instead she was detained and sent under guard to a forced labour camp to work as an agricultural labourer. On 5 September 1942 this world famous athlete was deported to an extermination camp at Rambula in Latvia where the camp policy was to starve inmates to death. Those who hung on to life for more than three days were shot. She was executed on 8 September 1942.

1937:   Speer appointed as 'Berlin's Inspector General of Buildings' and tasked with rebuilding Berlin as *Germania*.

1938:   Jews excluded from cinema, theatre, concerts, exhibitions, beaches and holiday resorts, and forced to add the names 'Sara', for women, or 'Israel', for men, to their own. In March, some 185,000 Jews lived in Austria when it was occupied and annexed by Germany; for days after the German take-over, Austrians engaged in a frenzy of violence and looting against the Jews. In panic, thousands tried to emigrate. About 130,000 Jews were able to leave, mostly passing through the Central Office for Jewish Emigration, an organisation established by SS lieutenant Adolf Eichmann. This office gave Jews the necessary exit papers, in return for which they were effectively stripped of all their assets and left as penniless refugees. Hundreds of Viennese Jews, despairing of the future and unable to emigrate, committed suicide.

On 13 June 'Gypsy clean-up week' was launched across Germany, and continued for a whole week. The police were issued with arrest quotas to fulfil, although only males capable of work were to be arrested. Once gathered, they were to be sent directly to concentration camps at Buchenwald, Dachau or Sachsenhausen. Apart from male Jews, any Sinti or Roma people that were found were to be arrested as part of the campaign. The date 9 November, better known as *Kristallnacht*, was a night of mass violence across Germany, fanned by the SA. Hundreds of German and Austrian Jews were murdered, 400 synagogues were burnt down, while others were desecrated. An estimated 7,000 Jewish-owned shops were plundered and their windows smashed. Thousands of Jews were arrested and Jewish children expelled from German schools.[4]

1939:   In April, regulations were promulgated under the Nuremberg Laws to enable local authorities across Germany to evict Jews from their homes, and to concentrate them in segregated housing. Enacted across Berlin, these laws enabled Speer's departments to evict Jewish tenants of non-Jewish landlords, ostensibly to make way for non-Jewish tenants displaced by redevelopment. Many of the finest properties were gifted by Speer as 'grace and favour' rewards, or bribes. Eventually, 75,000 Jews were displaced by such measures.

Speer denied he knew anything about these unfortunate people, displaced by his staff, before they were forcibly put on Holocaust trains and claimed that 'those displaced were completely free and their families were still in their apartments'.[5]

The historian Matthias Schmidt added a further comment by Speer:

> ... en route to my ministry on the city highway, I could see ... crowds of people on the platform of nearby Nikolassee Railroad Station. I knew that these must be Berlin Jews who were being evacuated. I am sure that an oppressive feeling struck me as I drove past. I presumably had a sense of sombre events.[6]

Schmidt said Speer had personally inspected concentration camps and described Speer's comments as an 'outright farce'.[7] As Germany started the Second World War in Europe, Speer instituted quick-reaction squads to construct roads or clear away debris; before long, these units would be used to clear bomb sites. Speer's officials used forced Jewish labour on these projects, in addition to regular German workers. Speer's offices undertook building work for each branch of the military, and for the SS, using slave labour. Speer's building work made him one of the wealthiest of the Nazi elite,[8] but by the war's end, this wealth evaporated through the devastating inflation that hit the country, leaving his family with few resources.

1940: Jews' telephones confiscated.

1941: In late July, Heinrich Himmler augmented the *Einsatzgruppen* (execution squads, operating mostly in Eastern Europe) by bringing in additional SS units and police battalions. These police consisted of elderly or recently retired German police officers, most with no military training. They began the mass shooting of Jews, including Jewish women and children held in concentration camps. A number of established Jewish communities, sometimes whole Jewish villages, were also annihilated. The Central Office for Jewish Emigration was set up, which required Jews' passports to be stamped with a red letter 'J', with many having their passports seized to prevent them leaving the country. Jews were evicted from their homes without reason or notice. Jews' radios were confiscated and a night-time curfew established. Jews no longer received ration cards for clothes. Jews over 6 years of age were forced to wear a yellow Star of David with 'Jew' written on it. Jews were forbidden to use public telephones or to keep dogs, cats or birds. In September the first concentration camp in Cologne was established in the city centre fairgrounds, the inmates were initially forced to clear bomb damage across the city.

1942:   During September, the eviction of remaining Jews from their homes was conducted across Germany. Many hundreds of Jews in Hannover received notices to evacuate their homes within twenty-four hours. They were only permitted to take essentials that could be carried, while the remainder of their possessions and property would be officially 'sold' and the proceeds turned over to them at a 'given time'. The mayor of Hannover issued a personal statement saying: 'In order to relieve the distressed situation caused by the war, I see myself compelled to immediately narrow down the space available to Jews in this city. I, therefore, demand that you quit your abode immediately.'

It is reported that one of the places of shelter assigned to the evicted Hannover Jews was the mortuary hall of a local Jewish cemetery. Jews were ordered to surrender their fur coats and woollen items. Jews were not allowed to receive eggs or milk. Blind or deaf Jews were no longer allowed to wear armbands identifying their condition. All schools were closed to Jewish children. Speer advocated using concentration camp prisoners and slave labour in factories, especially where such prisoners were qualified engineers. Many lived in or near their factories. The policy was approved by Hitler.

1943:   The year witnessed the continuous deportations of Jews. Concentration camp prisoners, mostly foreign slave labour and prisoners of war, were now being openly used across German cities to repair Allied bomb damage. They were farmed out from the many hundreds of camps now spread out across Germany; they lived in makeshift camps and were brutally treated, even in full view of the local population. When starved and unable to work, they were executed where they lay. One camp, the Cologne fairground, was notorious for its appalling public treatment of some 5,000 such prisoners, many of whom were visibly skeletal before dying from malnutrition; many were shot in the streets when too ill to work or exhausted. Such scenes were now common across Germany. For the German civilians, there was nothing they could say or do to assist such prisoners except to ignore what was happening before their eyes.[9] The year 1943 saw the police system of encouraging denunciations from the public, and funnelling them to the Gestapo, become widespread. Such denunciations were frequently from within families or work groups and most were acknowledged by the Gestapo as frivolous, to wreak revenge on someone or just out of jealousy, nevertheless, to maintain the flow of such information, arrests invariably followed with the majority resulting in swift executions. One case out of many tens of thousands highlights the weight of threat overhanging every German citizen; the senior manager of the Deutsche Bank was denounced by a member of staff for allegedly making a political comment. He was arrested and executed within days. For this case and a full review of denunciations, the complainants, their motivation and victims, see *Backing Hitler*.

1944:   In June, Hitler orders the implementation of his 'scorched earth' policy in front of the advancing Allies, with the intention of destroying all existing German industry. Speer disobeys the order substituting the word 'deactivation' for 'destruction'; in any event, the Germans lacked the means or manpower to fulfil this policy. Towards the end of the year, fuel for the military, and coal for industry, ceased to be produced due to constant Allied bombing. Millions of German civilians became homeless. The Allied invasion of Europe progressed into Germany. Speer ordered factories vital to the war effort, many staffed by concentration camp prisoners, to be closed or moved to central locations within Germany to prevent them falling into the hands of the advancing Russian army.

1945:   During early 1945 with the defeat of Germany imminent and in the depths of winter, concentration camps in the line of the approaching Allied troops were to be destroyed and their prisoners force marched away towards central Germany. Their intended collection camp was to be the isolated concentration camp at the village of Bergen-Belsen north of Hannover – their destiny was to be starved to death.

In the days before the German surrender, the Gestapo and police commandos set about slaughtering as many foreign workers as they could find, their bodies dumped in mass graves. Records indicate over 10,000 were executed with 90 per cent being foreigners, the remainder were those randomly considered suspicious.[10]

At his Nuremberg trial, Speer stated in his testimony 'All the sacrifices that were made, on both sides, from January 1945, were senseless.'

End of the Second World War.

1966: Speer released from Spandau Prison.

Following his release, and through his autobiographies and interviews, Speer carefully constructed an image of himself as a man who deeply regretted having failed to discover the monstrous crimes of the Third Reich. In particular, he continued to deny explicit knowledge of, and personal responsibility for, the Holocaust. This stance disregarded the fact that the *Schutzstaffel* (SS) built two concentration camps in 1938, and used the inmates to quarry stone for its construction, all approved of by Speer. A brick factory was built near the Oranienburg concentration camp at Speer's behest; when someone commented on the poor conditions there, Speer stated, 'The Yids got used to making bricks while in Egyptian captivity.'[11]

Persistent questions about Speer's truthfulness began to haunt him soon after his release. In 1971, Harvard University's Erich Goldhagen alleged that Speer had always been aware of the extermination of Jews. This was partly based on substantial evidence that Speer had attended a Nazi conference in 1943, at which Himmler had spoken openly about 'wiping the Jews from the face of the earth'. Speer originally admitted that he was present at the conference, but claimed he had left before Himmler gave his infamous 'Final Solution' speech, so therefore knew nothing about the matter. In later correspondence, consisting of letters between Speer to Hélène Jeanty, the widow of a Belgian resistance leader, there is an admission by Speer that he had indeed been present, and heard Himmler's speech about exterminating the Jews. Speer wrote: 'There is no doubt. I was present as Himmler announced on 6 October 1943 that all Jews would be killed.'[12]

Chapter Four

Why and How? An Insight into the German Attitude to Mass Murder between 1933 and 1945

During the early twentieth-century European grab for colonies in Africa, the 1904 uprising in German South-West Africa turned into a war of annihilation against the *Herero* peoples of Namibia. Namibia's senior German administrator, General Lothar von Trotha, issued an order that all *Herero* men should be executed, and women and children led into the desert to die; to speed the process German forces first destroyed the few wells in the desert. In October 1904, a rebellion of the *Namaqua* and *Saan* people followed, this also resulted in mass extermination by the German army. During this campaign, the Germans built one of their first concentration camps on a narrow peninsula known as Shark Island, a peninsula jutting into the Atlantic, where some 2,000 prisoners were starved, beaten and worked to death.

This brutal policy of containment continued during the occupation of German East Africa (Tanzania) where German troops systematically used brutality and mass murder of civilians to obtain domination. Other colonial powers looked more towards the civilization of their subject peoples whereas the Germans seemed comfortable with their civilization process being more influenced by its history of brutality. During their advance to France at the beginning of the First World War the invading German armies marched through Belgium and Holland systematically adopted looting, rape, arson, random shootings of civilians and the destruction of villages, towns and cities as permissible acts of war. These shocking acts were contrary to the Hague rules of war but there was then no way of bringing offenders to book for such conduct. By the end of the First World War it could well be the case that ordinary Germans accepted brutality to others in both a social and historical setting; social because they had long seen themselves as a superior people, and historically because the policy had previously helped their troops achieve domination. The policy was perpetuated in 1936 when a number of Spanish cities and towns were selected by the German military for indiscriminate bombing, resulting in significant damage and numerous deaths. This act was totally unexpected by the target's civilian populations, hence the high number of casualties. It was an action which met with widespread approval in Germany.

By the time Hitler rose to power, Germans were already familiar with the tactic of linking military aggression with brutality and ruthless oppression towards subjugated civilian populations, and by the time of the Second World War, they showed a willingness to accept this behaviour on a wide scale. Such a collective belief in their superiority might account for Germans later becoming such willing killers, especially when it came to their intended annihilation of Europe's widely despised Jews. And in the final days of the Second World War, with Germany defeated and millions of their people bewildered, starving and homeless, the Nazis turned their policy of murder to some 15,000 young German 'deserters' shell-shocked and wounded soldiers who had somehow survived the Russian destruction of their units, and been caught trying to get back to Germany. (See Ch.10. Reference 19).

Nevertheless, the question remains; how and why were Second World War Germans so willing to engage in the systematic slaughter of millions of unarmed defenceless people, including women and children, without pity, and with seeming gratification. No other country systematically built concentration or extermination camps or organised the enslavement of millions of subjected civilians to be worked to death in terrible conditions. The same question applies to the willingness, even enthusiasm, of normal German troops to participate in countless mass shootings of civilians and prisoners of war, mainly eastern European and Russians. Even if the participants were merely 'obeying orders', the facts suggest something deeper in the German psyche that 'orders must be obeyed'. Saying 'No' was somehow not an option for adherents of the dominating and complex 'obedience' factor, which, nevertheless, appears to be an important feature of the German national character. Whilst atrocities occurred throughout the war, such being the nature of warfare, the worst excesses by far were willingly committed on an industrial scale by Germans. Their soldiers frequently and unnecessarily burned down villages and towns and murdered whole populations including the elderly, women and children, to the extent that Russia lost twice as many civilians as their fighting military. When the Russians overran eastern Germany and then Berlin it was hardly a surprise they extracted terrible revenge on German prisoners of war by marching them to Russia's forced labour camps before turning their attention to the civilian population, especially the women.

This barbaric tyranny continued right to the end of the war when the surviving inmates of concentration camps were moved by their merciless guards out of the numerous extermination camps onto the infamous 'death marches' across Germany. This mindless action, in deep winter, was an attempt to hide the very existence and location of concentration camps and camp inmates from the advancing Allies. Local populations through which these desperate and starving columns painfully progressed rarely offered help, choosing instead to exhort their captors to move them away from their towns and villages.

In the final days of the war, the Gestapo staff and officials set fire to incriminating records all over the country while millions of former Nazis hid or burned their uniforms. But everyone knew something terrible had happened, though little was said, other than for individuals to deny knowledge of anything unsavoury. Not until the 1960s did doubts about the German nation's lack of knowledge of their country's treatment of prisoners and Jews, or of their participation in associated atrocities, slowly begin to emerge. It then became clear to researchers that details of mass deaths of Jews in concentration camps had long been well known across Germany, even publicized in local and national newspapers. For example, in 2001, according to Professor John Ezard:

> Ordinary Germans knew full well about the evolving terror of Hitler's Holocaust. They knew concentration camps were full of Jewish people who were stigmatised as sub-human and race-defilers. They knew that these, like other groups and minorities, were being killed out of hand, because they had read about them.

In research described as 'ground-breaking' by Oxford University Press, it is claimed the German people knew that Hitler had repeatedly forecast the extermination of every Jew on German soil, a policy made public in Hitler's *Mein Kampf*. They knew because the camps, and the measures that led up to them, had been prominently and proudly reported, step-by-step, in thousands of officially-inspired German media articles from the twenty-four main newspapers and magazines of the period.

The research is supported by Professor Robert Gellately in his book, *Backing Hitler*, which destroys the claim – generally made by Germans after

Berlin fell in 1945, and then accepted by most historians – that German civilians did not know about camp atrocities. Their collective amnesia ignored the fact that by the end of the war, hundreds of concentration camps were spread across the country, next to villages, towns and cities, and they were staffed by local Germans.

A leading British-born holocaust historian, Professor Michael Burleigh, said Gellately's book was 'original and outstanding, genuinely important'. Another authority on the camps, Professor Omer Bartov of Brown University, Rhode Island, US, described *Backing Hitler* as 'path-breaking – a crucial contribution to our understanding of the relationship between consent and coercion in modern dictatorship'. See Richard Gellately's *Backing Hitler* in which he wrote: 'For decades my generation had been told that so much of the terror had been carried out in complete secrecy.'

This broadening mission, as Gellately calls it, was reflected in the 1930s German newspaper *Volkische Beobachter*, when it published photographs of 'typical sub humans' including Jews with 'deformed head shapes'. For the first time the detention of the seriously disabled was said to be permanent. In January 1937, the newspaper *Berliner Borsen-Zeitung* reported the SS chief, Heinrich Himmler, announcing the need for 'still more camps for those with hydrocephalus, cross-eyed, deformed half-Jews, and a whole series of racially inferior types'.

German resistance

Not all Germans approved of Hitler's policies but they were helpless to openly voice their dissent. Some Germans did make a stand, and did so bravely, regardless of the obvious consequences of being arrested. Within Germany itself, the twelve year period leading up to 1945 recorded over 40,000 German civilians sentenced to death for 'offences' against the Nazi regime. Even voicing an opinion against the Nazis merited a death sentence. This recorded figure of over 40,000 victims was, by any account, an enormous number of executions of its own citizens in a modern country. For example, in 1943 three young non-violent medical students at Munich University, Hans and Sophie Scholl and a fellow student, Christoph Probst, deposited a suitcase on the university campus containing their home-produced 'White Rose' anti-Nazi leaflets. A suspicious janitor, who recognised the students, reported them to the Gestapo. Arrested and urgently questioned with the help of thumbscrews, the names of their close friends fell like autumn leaves which, under the rules of *Sippenhaft*, resulted in a further seventy of their fellow students and family members being arrested and interrogated. Within hours the three students were tried and sentenced to immediate death by guillotine, closely followed by their unsuspecting and innocent university tutor, Professor Huber. Those close to the three students were either sentenced to death by guillotine – the punishment reserved for political traitors, or sent to concentration camps. In southern Germany alone, more than 1,000 souls who voiced their opposition to the Nazis were executed at the Stadelheim Prison in Munich, with countless others killed in the nearby Dachau concentration camp, a former gunpowder factory.

My Opposition (German: *Mein Widerstand*) is a recently published diary secretly written during the Second World War by the German social democrat Friedrich Kellner (1885–1970) to describe life under Nazi Germany and to expose the propaganda and crimes of the Nazi dictatorship; it was discovered by his grandson after his death.

Friedrich Kellner was born in Mainz in 1885. During the Weimar Republic he started work as a junior court official while becoming an active Social Democrat in the Rhineland town of Mainz. The Social Democrats were then the mainstay of German democracy during the 1920s, but despite their millions of supporters, they proved unable to resist the Nazi seizure of power in 1933. By then, Kellner, a veteran of the First World War, was already an opponent of Hitler and the Nazi movement. A lifelong Social Democrat, he delivered a number of 'low-key' anti-Nazi speeches during the heady Weimar Republic years, for which he was often assaulted. Following the regime's *Kristallnacht* pogrom in 1938, thousands of Social Democrats were arrested and imprisoned. As a protest, Kellner put his name to a letter of support for the riot leaders, but in retaliation, a Nazi judge ordered that he and his wife's ancestry be investigated for traces of Jewish ancestry, with the obvious threat of imminent arrest and incarceration in the nearby concentration camp. To escape persecution, Kellner moved to Laubach, an alpine village in Upper Hesse, where he was unknown. He became the part-time administrator of the local courthouse. Clearly perceptive, he wrote in his diary on 17 December 1942:

Hitler is the most cunning criminal of all time … He is the bloodiest tyrant filled up with cruelty and unremitting hardness. He, who seduces, inveigles, lies to, and cheats the nation, has won millions of adherents and makes them into fanatical fighters for his heresies, which are nothing other than a conglomerate of ideas stolen from other fanatics.

Throughout the war, this brave and remarkable man continued to confide to his diary his moral outrage at the crimes of the regime, and his contempt for the gullible Germans who accepted them and believed in Hitler's lies. His diary was later discovered and published by his grandson, but not until after his death in 1970. Among many other crimes, he wrote about the 'mercy killings' of disabled Germans at Hadamar, and 'retribution' killings carried out against civilians in occupied countries. He added: 'Because ninety-nine percent of the German population is guilty, directly or indirectly, for the present situation, we can only say that those who travel together will hang together.'

Following the liberation of Germany, Kellner was appointed deputy mayor of Laubach, where he helped with de-Nazification and to revive the Social Democratic Party. He died in 1970, long before his *My Opposition* diary came to the attention of the public. The full diary was not published in Germany until 2011.

The major participants, Germans, Jews and the Allies, all believed in God, yet no religious leader in Germany made a stand against the Nazi Party or its treatment and extermination of the Jews. See *Hitler's Willing Executioners* Goldhagen, Daniel (Abacus, 1997).

At the end of the war, those considered most responsible, and who could be found, had to answer for their actions. For the rest of the German population, a schism quickly took hold between the immersion in their self-made misery as victims and their wish to forget what they had so determinedly and enthusiastically inflicted on the defeated peoples of Europe and Russia.

Chapter Five

The Nuremberg Trials of the International Military Tribunal 1945 to 1949

'His appearance was striking, even in prison clothes.'
Nuremberg prosecutor.

Nuremberg in southern Germany was selected as the venue for the first war crimes trial that commenced in 1945; numerous other trials followed. All four Allied powers appointed their top judges under the auspices of the International Military Tribunal, who presided over the trials of the twenty-one most senior Nazis; twelve of whom were sentenced to death. Crimes with which the accused were charged excluded the many crimes committed against the German people; theoretically, these would be dealt with by German courts, but were mostly ignored by the new and overwhelmed German authorities trying to regain some semblance of civil order.

The purpose of the first of this series of trials was to bring the most senior German war criminals, including Albert Speer, to justice. The trials took place on the instruction of the Allied governments at the end of the Second World War. The most significant trial was the first, where the top members of the Nazi Party were prosecuted, according to international law and the laws of war. Political authority for the trials was granted under the Allied Control Council, this gave the judges the right to punish offences against international law and the laws of war.

Because the court was limited to war crimes, it had no jurisdiction over crimes committed before the outbreak of war on 1 September 1939.

There are many authoritative books and research papers about this famous trial. The full transcripts and recordings of all the Nuremberg trials are in the public domain and do not contribute to this specific account. However, a short timeline and the inclusion of sections specifically relating to Albert Speer, which are not readily accessed for public viewing elsewhere, may be helpful. At the outset of the trial it was made clear that the stated aim of the trials was not to incriminate the whole German people.

Even while under initial arrest, mostly in solitary confinement, Speer was supremely confident he would have an important role in post-war Germany; after all, he was the expert on German industry and armament production. Since his arrest he had been well treated, as had the German rocket expert, Wernher von Braun; both had freely volunteered to work and cooperate with the Allies, who were very keen to discover Germany's military secrets. Shortly following their arrests, these special prisoners were assessed with a number of psychological tests; their IQ results are illuminating and are shown in brackets.

Dönitz, Karl, Admiral of the Fleet (138).

Frank, Hans, Politician and lawyer, head of the General Government in Poland (130).

Frick, Wilhelm, Last governor of the Protectorate of Bohemia and Moravia (124).

Fritzch, Hans, Ministerial director at the Propaganda Ministry (130).

Funk, Walther, Economics minister and president of the Reichsbank (124).

Goering, Herman, German political and military leader (138).

Hess, Rudolf, Deputy Führer (120).

Jodl, Alfred, Chief of the Operations Staff of the Armed Forces High Command (127).

Kaltenbrunner, Ernst, Chief of the Reich Main Security Office (113).

Keitel, Wilhelm, Field Marshal. Ordered unprecedented brutality and criminality (129).

Neurath, Konstantin, German diplomat, served as Foreign Minister of Germany (125).

Papen, Franz, Vice-Chancellor under Adolf Hitler in 1933–34 (134).

Raeder, Erich, German Admiral (134).

Ribbentrop, Joachim, German Foreign Minister from 1938 until 1945 (129).

Rosenberg, Alfred, Reich Ministry for the Occupied Eastern Territories (127).

Sauckel, Fritz, General Plenipotentiary for Labour Deployment (118).

Schacht, Hjalmar, Currency Commissioner and President of the Reichsbank (143).

Schirach, Baldur, Hitler Youth leader and *Gauleiter* of Vienna (130).

Seyss-Inquart, Arthur, *Reichskommissar* (Commissioner) of the occupied Netherlands (141).

Speer, Albert, Architect and Minister of Production (128).

Streicher, Julius, Editor of the anti-Semitic newspaper *Der Störmer* (106).

After Speer had been assessed he claimed to have played games with the psychologists, so his assessment was deemed to be unreliable, or was he disappointed with his score? In any event, it came as a huge shock to Speer to be included on the list of major war criminals to be tried for war crimes. Instead of helping the Allies to rebuild Germany, as he had anticipated, he was to be tried alongside the worst Nazi criminals; he and his co-defendants would collectively face four charges:

i.   Engaged in a criminal conspiracy; to accomplish the planning or waging a war of aggression, or war in violation of international treaties, agreements or assurances.
ii. Crimes against peace; planning, preparing, initiating or waging of a war of aggression, or a war in violation of international treaties.
iii. War crimes; violations of the laws or customs of war, to include murder, ill-treatment or deportation to slave labour or for any other purpose, of civilian populations, prisoners of war, persons on the seas, killing of hostages, plunder, wanton destruction not justified by military necessity.
iv. Crimes against humanity; murder, extermination, enslavement, deportation and other inhumane acts committed against any civilian, before or during the war, or persecution on political, racial or religious grounds, in connection with any crime within the jurisdiction of the Tribunal.

The trial opened on the 20 November 1945, tediously for the defendants, commencing with all the necessary formalities and procedures that accompany the beginning of a major prosecution. Then, on 29 November, a week into the trial, there was a dramatic change in the tone of the proceedings when

Chief United States Prosecutor Robert Jackson opened the trial by showing an hour-long German-made film titled *Nazi Concentration Camps*. Jackson started the film with the words 'We will show you their own films'.

For many years, the Germans enthusiastically filmed their activities and events, to the extent that they made dedicated filming of events and daily life, and especially military activities, a priority, even of its worst excesses in concentration camps. From the earliest beginnings of the Nazi Party in the 1920s, and all through the military invasions of the Second World War, German camera crews recorded (often proudly) graphic depictions of atrocities. In a chilly courtroom on a cold and grey November day, the ghastly impact of such visual evidence brought the Holocaust into the silent courtroom and appalled everyone, including the defendants, who appeared equally shocked. All of the accused now realised that the film had shockingly set the tone for their trial. In consequence, the defendants now fully understood the magnitude of the situation they found themselves in; indeed, their very lives were on the line, and there could be little mercy. Robert Jackson, the Representative and Chief of Counsel for the United States of America then stated:

> This war did not just happen – it was planned and prepared for over a long period of time and with no small skill and cunning. The world has perhaps never seen such a concentration and stimulation of the energies of any people as that which enabled Germany 20 years after it was defeated, disarmed, and dismembered to come so near to carrying out its plan to dominate Europe.

As the trial progressed, a further film made by the Russian prosecutors was shown on 19 February 1946, titled *Cruelties of the German-Fascist Intruders*, detailing the results of atrocities in the extermination camps discovered by Russian troops. There was no let-up in the thrust of the trial.

From the outset of the trial, Speer alone, almost over-willingly accepted responsibility for following Hitler's orders. He later confirmed his culpability in his book, *Secret Diaries*, by writing:

> I assumed responsibility for all the orders from Hitler which I carried out. I took the position that in every government, orders must remain orders for the subordinate organs of the government, but that the leadership on all levels must examine and weigh the orders it receives

and is consequently co-responsible for them, even if the orders have been carried out under duress.

What mattered more to me was to exert my collective responsibility for all the measures of Hitler, not excluding the crimes, which were undertaken or committed in the period from 1942 on wherever and by whom.

He willingly confirmed his position before the court, stating:

In political life there is a responsibility for a man's own sector. For that he is of course responsible. But beyond that there is a collective responsibility when he has been one of the leaders. Who else is to be held responsible for the course of events, if not the closest associates of the Chief of State? But this collective can only apply to fundamental matter and not to details. Even in an authoritarian system this collective responsibility of the leaders must exist; there can be no attempting to withdraw from the collective responsibility after the catastrophe. For if the war had been won, the leadership would probably have raised the claim that it was collectively responsible.[1]

British Major Airey Neave, a 29-year-old lawyer, fluent in German, and a Colditz escapee, was part of the British prosecution team under Hartley William Shawcross (Baron Shawcross, GBE, PC, QC), a British barrister and the lead British prosecutor at the trials. Neave helped prepare the case against Speer, and later commented that Speer was initially an impressive figure, a gifted and talented man. He wrote:

His appearance was striking, even in prison clothes. He was tall and dark with a strong intelligent face and thoughtful eyes. His manner was of an athletic university professor who had turned to public service. He was, I felt, a man of considerable distinction. However, I felt repelled by his smoothness, he was, I felt, more beguiling and dangerous than Hitler who had died before in the ruins of Berlin.

The trial lasted 260 days before the judges summed up the evidence. With regard to Speer, they stated that for crimes against peace, they were of the collective opinion that:

Speer's activities did not amount to initiating planning, or preparing wars of aggression, or of conspiring to that end. He became the head of the armament industry well after all of the wars had been commenced and were underway. His activities in charge of German Armament Production were in aid of the war effort in the same way that other productive enterprises aid in the waging of war, but the Tribunal is not prepared to find that such activities involve engaging in the common plan to wage aggressive war as charged under Count I or waging aggressive war as charged under Count II.

The gist of the evidence against Speer under Counts III and IV related entirely to his participation in the slave labour programme and elicited the following statement from the prosecutor:

Speer was directly involved in the utilisation of forced labour as Chief of the Organisation Todt. The Organisation Todt functioned principally in the occupied areas on such projects as the Atlantic Wall and the construction of military highways, and Speer has admitted that he relied on compulsory service to keep it adequately staffed. He also used concentration camp labour in the industries under his control. He originally arranged to tap this source of labour for use in small out of the way factories, and later, fearful of Himmler's jurisdictional ambitions, attempted to use as few concentration camp workers as possible. Speer was also involved in the use of prisoners of war in armament industries but contends that he only utilised Soviet prisoners of war in industries covered by the Geneva Convention. Speer's position was such that he was not directly concerned with the cruelty in the administration of the slave labour programme, although he was aware of its existence.

The Court published a pre-sentence statement dealing with Speer which reads:

After all complications of trial and retrial which may occur, as well as the possible appeal, the trial(s) of Albert Speer in the International Criminal Court will essentially boil down to one of four options. Either, the court eventually will decide to

a. release him,
b. the court will place the man under discussed probation,

c. the court will imprison him for a determined duration of time, or
d. the court can rule to put him to death.

In order for all charges to be lifted from Albert Speer, and the man be released, the defence would have to present a case in which the man charged is found innocent. The defence will be wise to remember that the defendant is innocent until proven guilty. There has to be no reasonable doubt in order for the man to be innocent, however. Another possibility is that the court will rule to place Speer under probation. The terms of the probation will be discussed and determined by those in the court and final ruling will be given by the judge(s). Speer can be imprisoned for his crimes. The sentence length will be discussed and determined by those in the court and the final ruling will be given by the judges. Finally, Speer can be given the death penalty. The man's crimes will have been found severe enough to justify taking his life. The final ruling and method by which Albert Speer will be put to death will be determined by the judges.

On 31 August, the final day of the trial, all defendants were allowed to address the Court with a statement not previously submitted to the court. Albert Speer addressed the court, in German, as follows (author's translation):

Mr President and members of the court.

Hitler and the collapse of his regime has brought an incredible time of suffering for the German people.

The useless continuation of the war and the unnecessary destruction makes the reconstruction to be a very hard task. Privation and misery have come over the German people. It (Germany) will, after this process, despise and condemn Hitler as the proven author of its misfortune, but the world will learn from what happened, not only to hate the dictatorship as a form of government, but also to fear it.

What means my own destiny, after all, what happened and in regards of such high purpose? The German people did in earlier centuries contribute much to the development of human culture. It often has brought these contributions in times when it was just as powerless and helpless as it is today. Valuable people don't let themselves be driven to despair, but a people that believes in its future will not be lost.

God save Germany and the Western culture.

On 1 October that same year, the Tribunal found that Speer was not guilty on Counts I and II, but guilty under counts III and IV relating to war crimes and crimes against humanity, principally for the use of slave labour under his direction.

Speer narrowly escaped the death sentence; the Russian judges unanimously voted to execute him, but they were marginally overruled by the other judges. Instead, he was sentenced to twenty years' imprisonment for his perceived war crimes carried out during the Second World War; although Lord Shawcross later commented that it was wrong that Speer was treated leniently while his deputy, the arrogant Fritz Sauckel, ever antagonistic towards the judges until the end of the trial, went to the gallows for obeying Speer's orders. Speer later wrote, 'In this world, adaptability and cunning carry you a lot farther.'[2]

The following were sentenced to death by hanging
Goering, Ribbentrop, Keitel, Kaltenbrunner, Rosenberg, Frank, Frick, Streicher, Sauckel, Jodl, and Seyss-Inquart. Goering managed to commit suicide prior to his execution by taking cyanide, which he had arranged to have smuggled to him. Those sentenced to death were executed by hanging in the early hours of 16 October 1946.

The following were sentenced to imprisonment
Hess, Funk, Raeder: Life, Neurath: 15 years, Schirach and Speer: 20 years. Dönitz was sentenced to 10 years. Later, on the morning of the executions, these seven survivors were ordered to clean and clear the executed men's cells and wash the floor of the gymnasium where the hangings had taken place.

To the judges, Speer was at least guilty of 'turning a blind eye', having been well aware of the mistreatment of his prisoner-workers. With regard to other crimes against humanity, Speer had somewhat arrogantly insisted, 'the German people do not do such things.' He added, 'In an authoritarian system one engages in the politics if one wishes to remain among the leaders. I was a bureaucrat trapped by the politics.'[3]

Hjalmar Schacht, the Reich finance minister, was even more adept at escaping difficulties than Speer; he escaped conviction.[4]

On 10 October 1946, Speer's automatic appeal to the Control Council was rejected.

The executions did not proceed smoothly. In autumn 1944, the American Army in Germany advertised for a volunteer hangman. GI John C. Woods volunteered and falsely claimed to have been a hangman in both Texas and Oklahoma. Woods was then serving with the 37th Engineer Combat Battalion. He had no credentials and none were requested. He was accepted for the position and transferred to the Paris Disciplinary Training Centre where he performed the hangings of a number of convicted American soldiers. US Army reports reveal that most, eleven in all, were considered to have been bungled hangings. Nevertheless, his competence was not challenged; the hangings had, somehow, been achieved, and the necessary death certificates issued, and that was all that was required of the law. Woods was then sent to Nuremberg as the official American executioner, and promoted to Master Sergeant for the role.

Commencing just after midnight on 16 October 1946, the names of the ten convicted Nazis sentenced to death were called out and the convicts were taken from their cells, one at a time, to be despatched by Woods on a makeshift gallows constructed on the ground floor of the prison gymnasium. Speer wrote:

I could hear footsteps and indistinguishable words in the lower hall. Then silence, broken by another name being called out. A cell door is opened, then scraps of phrases, scraping of boots and reverberating footsteps slowly fading away... Below, the calling of names goes on. I cannot estimate the time; it may be taking hours.

Speer's comment tends to corroborate the length of time taken by Woods to despatch the ten men, ordinarily a swift process. According to original archives:

The inexperienced Army hangman, Master Sgt. John C. Woods, botched the executions. A number of the hanged Nazis died, not quickly from a broken neck as intended, but agonizingly from slow strangulation. Ribbentrop and Sauckel each took 14 minutes to choke to death, while Keitel, whose death was the most painful, struggled for 28 minutes at the end of the rope before expiring.[5]

Woods went on to conduct the executions of another forty-five war criminals at various prison locations, which included Bruchsal, Landsberg and Rheinbach. But suspicions had been raised, and subsequent enquiries of Wood's experience revealed, not only his big lie, but also that he had previously been diagnosed by the US Navy with 'Constitutional Psychopathic Inferiority without Psychosis'. He was found unfit for military service and discharged from the Navy, but he was then recruited into the US Army in 1943. Following his tour as the US military executioner, he settled in Germany and died soon afterwards from an unexplained electrocution while working for a local German company.[6]

Another 185 people were indicted in the subsequent Nuremberg trials; 12 defendants received death sentences, 8 others were given prison life sentences and 77 people received prison terms of varying lengths.

Further courts then assembled across Germany, under the same authority, to try categorised defendants in separate trials, which included:

Doctors, for which 23 defendants were accused of crimes against humanity, including medical experiments on prisoners of war.

Foreign Ministry officials.

Lawyers and judges, of which 16 lawyers were charged with furthering the Nazi plan for racial purity by implementing the Nazis eugenics laws.

SS officers for war crimes or violence against concentration-camp inmates.

Senior army officers accused of atrocities against prisoners of war.

German industrialists accused of using slave labour and plundering occupied countries.

In late 1945, Albert Pierrepoint, the official British war crimes executioner, was sent to Hameln (Hamlin) in northern Germany; the concentration camp at Bergen-Belsen was nearby and the subsequent trial of the camp's officials and functionaries resulted in a number of camp officials being sentenced to death. He was to carry out the executions of eleven of those sentenced plus two Germans convicted of murdering an RAF pilot. Pierrepoint was given the honorary military rank of Lieutenant Colonel, but General Montgomery inadvertently let slip Pierrepoint's name, so that when he arrived in Germany, he was constantly followed by the press. On 13 December, he first individually executed several women, then the men two at a time. Pierrepoint travelled several times to Hameln. Between December 1948 and October 1949 he alone executed 226 prisoners, sometimes 10 a day.

Among the other important trials conducted after the first Nuremberg trial, the following concentration camp trials also took place:

• Auschwitz.
• Bergen-Belsen.
• Belzec. Took place before the 1st Munich District Court in the mid-1960s; eight SS men of the Belzec extermination camp were tried.
• Chełmno. The trials took place in Poland and Germany. The cases of camp personnel were decided over a period of twenty years.
• Dachau.
• Frankfurt Auschwitz.
• Majdanek. The longest Nazi war crimes trials in history, spanning over thirty years.
• Mauthausen-Gusen.
• Hamburg Ravensbrück.
• Sobibór. Held in Hagen, Germany, in 1965 against the SS men of the Sobibór extermination camp.
• Treblinka trials held in Düsseldorf, Germany.

At the close of the Second World War, the hunt began for Germany's concentration camp staff. Of those arrested at the time of various camps being liberated by the Allies, many of these camp staffs were killed by vengeful inmates or angry Allied soldiers. Of those who initially escaped, many were later tracked down from surviving records kept by camp officials, then arrested and tried for murder and acts of brutality against their prisoners. Overall, an estimated 20,000 camp staff were eventually arrested for crimes committed; of these, more than 500 were sentenced to death at formal hearings, with the majority executed. Most concentration-camp commandants were caught, and in most cases received the death penalty. It is notable that in a high proportion of cases, it was the junior camp officials who were first caught, tried and in the worst cases, executed. An estimated 3,500 women camp officials were traced, but most of these evaded retribution, due, in part, to a lack of surviving witnesses. Several hundred of the most infamous women concentration camp offenders were traced; the very worst, some 65 in all, stood trial before War Crimes Tribunals. Of these, 21 were executed.

On 18 July 1947, Speer and the other six prisoners were flown to Berlin and transferred to Spandau Prison.[7]

Chapter Six

Spandau Prison, West Berlin

Built in 1876, and demolished in 1987, the red-brick Spandau Prison (Spandau) was located in the Spandau district of West Berlin, close to the long main road that crosses the city from west to east, the *Wilhelmstraße*. The prison had a grim and chequered history; during the Franco-Prussian war it served as a military detention centre. From 1919 it was used for civilian and political prisoners, frequently with up to 600 inmates, its capacity at that time. During the 1930s it was operated by the Prussian Ministry of Justice, before becoming infamous as one of the original 'concentration' camps for Berlin.

Spandau then entered an even darker period. Taken over by the Gestapo, they regularly used it for executions, or torture to the point of death to extract information from suspects and prison inmates. Under a particularly cruel Nazi law, known as *Sippenhaft* (guilt by association), an accused's family or associates could be considered equally guilty and treated similarly. For example, in the case of the failed 20 July 1944 attempt on Hitler's life by Count von Stauffenberg, Stauffenberg was immediately arrested at Berlin's army headquarters, taken into the courtyard then shot.[1] Within hours, Himmler ordered the arrest of all Stauffenberg's relatives, from his four infant children, to army colleagues and distant cousins. Some 600 of his family, friends and associates were then rounded up, interrogated and many were executed within hours. His heavily-pregnant wife, Countess Nina Stauffenberg, was nevertheless interrogated, then held in solitary confinement in Berlin, before being transferred to the Ravensbrück concentration camp, as was her mother, who subsequently perished there as a camp prisoner. The four young Stauffenberg children, the eldest was aged 10, were split up and placed in state orphanages in Thuringia, and given new, less-pretentious surnames to hide their identity. In January 1945, Nina Stauffenberg gave birth in a Nazi maternity home near Ravensbrück to her late husband's daughter, Konstanze. At the end of the war, the Countess was held as a prominent hostage by Ravensbrück camp guards, and although her guards had orders to kill her, they allowed her to be liberated by Allied troops in exchange for their safety. Because Ravensbrück had kept meticulous records of all their prisoners, the children could be traced and they and their mother were eventually reunited as a family. Stauffenberg's elder brother, Berthold Graf von Stauffenberg, a distinguished German aristocrat and lawyer, had also been presumed by the Gestapo to have been a supportive conspirator to assassinate Hitler. Following his arrest and lengthy interrogation he was executed by hanging.

Summary executions in Spandau were a regular feature; most were carried out by hanging, some by guillotine. The prison's purpose-built execution hall featured a foot-wide, 5-inch- deep gully, running the length of the chamber, before emptying into an outside drain to flush the room of execution victims' blood and body fluids. Gestapo and SS executions involved hanging the victim with thin wire, their hands tied behind their backs, with the victim suspended just inches from the floor. This resulted in a slow excruciating death that could last several minutes. The inevitable gossip from the prison guards about the 'twitching' of those dying soon became well-known across Berlin, and gave rise to the expression 'Spandau Ballet'. Those about to be executed would be cruelly forced to watch those ahead being put to death.

When, at the end of the Second World War, the Russians swept through Berlin, they found Spandau Prison unoccupied. From November 1945 until October 1946, the International Military War Crimes Tribunal at Nuremberg charged and prosecuted Nazi leaders for their roles in the Holocaust, and other crimes against humanity. Spandau Prison, located in the British Sector next to Brooke Barracks, home of the Welch Regiment, was prepared for the Allies' prisoners to serve their sentences; it was ideal as it gave the Russians easy access, without granting them any rights to enter West Germany.

During the first Nuremberg trials, it was anticipated that over 100 of the most senior war criminals would need to be imprisoned in Spandau. Plans were prepared and agreed by the four governing powers, but unfortunately for many of the prisoners, most unexpectedly received the death sentence, and went to the gallows on 16 October 1946. The death sentences were carried out in the gymnasium of Nuremberg Prison. Overall, 288 war criminals were condemned to death; 259 death sentences were conducted by hanging and 29 by firing squad. Unclaimed bodies were buried in unmarked graves in the cemetery next to the Spöttingen Chapel. For the numerous less important war criminals, convicted of crimes against humanity at the

Dachau trials and Nuremberg, the US Army designated War Criminal Prison No. 1 at Landsberg as a suitable prison. It was infamous for originally incarcerating Hitler following his failed 1923 *putsch*, and was administered and guarded by personnel from the United States Military Police. It housed war criminals who had earlier been formally sentenced to death, or long terms of imprisonment at other war crimes trials, and were awaiting execution or transfer elsewhere. In May 1946, twenty-eight former SS guards from Dachau were hanged within a four-day period. Many hundreds of other Germans, mostly concentration camp guards, were summarily executed by the Americans, a topic well-documented and not relevant to this account.

Of the twenty-four most senior Nazis who were show-trialled as major war criminals at Nuremberg, eleven were given the death penalty and executed; those with prison sentences were sent to Landsberg Prison, leaving just the seven most senior, and famous, but less culpable of inhuman war crimes to serve long prison sentences in Spandau. They were:

Baldur von Schirach, Hitler Youth, prisoner number one, 20 years.

Erich Raeder, admiral and chief of the German Navy, number two, Life.

Konstantin von Neurath, foreign minister, number three, 15 years.

Karl Dönitz, admiral, number four, 10 years.

Albert Speer, minister of production, number five, 20 years.

Walther Funk, Nazi economic minister, number six, Life.

Rudolf Hess, Hitler's deputy, number seven, Life.

These seven high-ranking Nazis finally arrived at Spandau by air from Nuremberg on 18 July 1947. Ready for them were sixty or so soldiers for guard duty around the prison perimeter, and a duty military officer; all were drawn from the regiments then serving in West Berlin. The Russian guards were transported to the prison by coaches from bases in East Berlin. Inside the prison were teams of professional civilian warders from each of the four countries, along with four senior prison Governors and their deputies, four army medical officers, cooks, translators, waiters, porters and others. Guarding the prison was soon perceived to be a drastic misallocation of resources for just seven prisoners, and became a serious point of contention among the prison directors and politicians from their respective countries. It was also decreed that the West Berlin government would meet all prison costs, other than costs to the military. The operation was run by the Kommandatura, the post-war governing body of Berlin, administered jointly by the US, UK, USSR and France, on a monthly rota of prison Governors and their staff, under the authority of the Four-Power Authorities.

Spandau was one of only two Four-Power organisations to continue to operate after the breakdown of the Allied Control Council; the other was the Berlin Air Safety Centre. The four occupying powers of Berlin alternated control of the prison on a monthly basis, each having the responsibility for a total of three months out of the year. By observing the duty nation's flag that flew over the building, a passer-by could determine who controlled the prison.

The prison itself, originally designed for a population in the high hundreds, was a castle-like old red-brick prison enclosed by one inner wall 15 feet high, another outer wall twice as high. This wall was topped with electrified wire, and reinforced by a further layer of barbed wire. In addition, six of the contingent of thirty armed soldiers on guard duty manned each of the six guard towers, twenty-four hours a day. Within the prison walls the only refuge for the inmates was the inner prison garden. It was spacious, given the small number of prisoners using it. Once the prisoners had settled into prison life, the garden was initially divided into small personal plots that were used by each prisoner in various ways, usually for the growing of vegetables. Dönitz favoured growing beans, Funk, tomatoes and Speer, daisies; although, for no apparent reason, the Soviet director banned flowers for a time. By regulation, all produce was put towards use in the prison kitchen, but prisoners and guards alike often ignored this particular rule and indulged in the garden's offerings to assuage their hunger, especially when the Russians were on duty; their meals were repetitive and inadequate to the extent that prisoners lost weight during each Russian tour of duty. As prison regulations slackened and prisoners became either apathetic or too ill to maintain their plots, the garden was consolidated into one large workable area. This suited the former architect Speer, who, being one of the youngest and liveliest of the inmates, took up the task of refashioning the entire plot of land into a large complex garden complete with paths, rock gardens and floral displays. On days without access to the garden, for instance when it was raining, the prisoners occupied their time with reading or making envelopes together in the main corridor.

In advance of the prisoners' arrival, every facet of prison life was strictly set out in intricate prison regulations. These had been specifically designed, and agreed by the Four Powers; Spandau's rules were strict, harsh and without compassion. The prisoners' outgoing letters to families were at first limited to one page each month, talking with fellow prisoners was prohibited, newspapers were initially banned, and later, had large sections cut out to prevent them following German politics. Diaries and memoirs were forbidden, visits by families were limited to fifteen minutes every two months, and lights were flashed into the prisoners' cells every fifteen minutes throughout the night to dissuade any prisoner from committing suicide. A considerable portion of the more strict regulations was either later revised toward the more lenient, or deliberately ignored by prison staff. The directors and guards of the Western powers repeatedly voiced opposition of the stricter measures and submitted regular protests about them to their superiors, but they were invariably vetoed by the Russians, who insisted on the original strict approach. The Russian position was understandable; they had suffered 19 million civilian deaths during the war and had pressed at the Nuremberg trials for the execution of all the current inmates. They were also unwilling to compromise with the Western powers, both because of the harsher punishments that they felt were justified, and to stress the Communist propaganda line, that their Allies had supposedly never been serious about de-Nazification. They also knew post-war plans had been considered by the Allies for an immediate joint German and Allied thrust eastwards to prevent Russia taking over Eastern Europe. Therefore, life in Berlin's Spandau Prison contrasted with Landsberg Prison in southern Germany, which saw many hundreds of convicted Nazi officers, officials and other lower-ranking men serving their prison sentences under a comparatively lax regime, which included early release for good behaviour.

Daily life at Spandau lacked any variety; every day, the prisoners were ordered to rise at 6.00 am, wash, clean their cells, and then wash the main corridor, all before breakfast. They could then, weather permitting, spend time in the garden until lunch then rest in their cells before returning to the garden. Supper followed at 5.00 pm after which the prisoners were returned to their cells. Lights went out at 10.00 pm. Prisoners could have a shave and a haircut every Monday, Wednesday and Friday and wash their laundry every Monday. This routine, except the time allowed in the garden, changed very little throughout the years, although each of the controlling nations practised their own interpretation of prison regulations.

Communications between the prisoners and the outside world were initially banned, but soon after the prisoners' arrival at Spandau, a few of the staff secretly assisted any prisoner wanting to establish contact with the outside world. These communications invariably relied on the use of toilet paper, as every other piece of paper given to the prisoners was recorded and tracked. Fortunately for those involved, the supply of toilet paper went unmonitored for the entire duration of the prisoners' existence. Albert Speer, after having his official request to write his memoirs denied, finally began setting down his experiences and perspectives of his time with the Nazi regime, which were smuggled out and later released as a bestselling book, *Inside the Third Reich*. Dönitz wrote letters to his former deputy regarding the protection of his prestige in the outside world. When his release was near, he gave instructions to his wife on how best she could help ease his transition back into politics, which he intended, but never actually accomplished. Walther Funk somehow managed to obtain a seemingly constant supply of cognac (all alcohol was banned) and other treats that he would share with his fellow prisoners on special occasions.

All prisoners dreaded the month when the Russians took command; they were strict in their enforcement of prison regulations and provided poor quality meals. Each nation in charge would bring its own chef; during the American, French, and British months, the prisoners were better fed than regulations called for. The Soviets, by contrast, provided an unchanging daily diet of coffee, bread, cabbage soup, and potatoes. This rigidity was primarily due to the much-loathed Soviet prison director, who perpetually enforced these measures, and whom Soviet and Western guards alike feared and despised. This director was suddenly removed in the early 1960s. Afterwards, many matters, including diet, were improved.

The prisoners persisted in continuing the petty personal rivalries between themselves, and subtle battles for prestige that had characterized Nazi Party politics. Cliques appeared, but Speer and Hess were avoided; the former for his admission of guilt and repudiation of Hitler at the Nuremberg trials, the latter for his antisocial personality and perceived mental instability. The two former Grand Admirals, Raeder and Dönitz, soon bonded together. Schirach and Funk became firm friends; Neurath being a former diplomat, was amiable to everyone. Despite the length of time they spent with each other, remarkably little progress was made in the way of any reconciliation within the group. A notable example was Dönitz's dislike of Speer, which he steadfastly maintained for his entire ten-year sentence, with it only coming to a head during the last few days of his imprisonment. Dönitz always believed, wrongly, that Hitler had named him as his successor on Speer's recommendation, which had led to Dönitz being tried at Nuremberg.

Of the seven, three were released after serving their full sentences, while three others, including Raeder and Funk, who were given life sentences, were released earlier due to ill health. In 1966 matters came to a head following the release of Speer and Schirach on the full completion of their twenty-year sentences, leaving Rudolf Hess, the only inmate in the prison. For purely humanitarian reasons, Western leaders proposed to release Hess from Spandau and place him in prison elsewhere, or hold him under secure house arrest. The Russians refused; had Hess been released or moved to West Germany, the Russians would have forgone their legal right of entry into West Berlin in order to fulfil their guard and prison duties. Western leaders and public pressure accused the Russians of keeping Spandau in operation, solely as a base for Soviet espionage operations in West Berlin. Certainly, without access to Spandau Prison, the Russians had no legal right to enter West Berlin. For the next twenty-one years, Hess remained in isolation, but the Russian position is understandable; while en route in their buses to the prison, they could familiarise countless Russian troops with the layout of West Berlin and Allied barracks.

Rudolf Hess then became the sole occupant in a facility designed to hold 600 prisoners. For seventeen years, his sole companion was the American warder, Eugene K. Bird, who did his best to befriend his charge. As the prison's only inmate, he was a long way removed from having been the second most powerful man in Germany, and Deputy Führer to Adolf Hitler. Bird saw Hess's every move and action, won his confidence, talked daily with him, and kept a day-to-day record that was later published as *The Loneliest Man in the World*.

Lord James Douglas-Hamilton (Edinburgh, West) raised the matter before Parliament with the following statement:

Hess has spent 34 years in captivity, 30 of them in Spandau. That is a long period of imprisonment by any standards. The last 9½ years have been spent in solitary confinement. Nine and a half years in solitary confinement is a barbarous form of punishment. I hope that the Minister will be as direct as Sir Winston Churchill was when he wrote:

'Reflecting upon the whole of this story, I am glad not to be responsible for the way in which Hess has been and is being treated. I hope that the Minister can take this matter up once more, together with the French and American Governments, in the hope of eliciting a reply from the Soviet Government.'

On 17 August 1987, at the age of 93, Hess allegedly committed suicide and Spandau Prison's last occupant was gone. To prevent the prison from becoming a neo-Nazi shrine, it was totally demolished, with all the rubble being dumped in the North Sea or buried at the former RAF Gatow airbase. All that remains is a single set of warders' keys, which can be seen in the regimental museum of the King's Own Scottish Borderers at Berwick Barracks.

As of 2006, and to further ensure its erasure, the prison site was made into a parking facility alongside a British Forces shopping centre, imaginatively named the Britannia Centre Spandau, and nicknamed 'Hesco'. In 2011 a development company applied for permission to demolish the complex. On 20 June 2013, a Kaufland supermarket opened on the site.

Oddly, four times in the twentieth-century, the date of 9 November has witnessed dramatic events in the history of Germany and Berlin. On that date in 1918, Berlin became the capital of the first German republic. Five years later, Hitler's *putsch* was put down in Munich. In 1938 Nazi storm troopers vandalized Jewish synagogues, shops, and other properties in the night of violence known as *Kristallnacht* (Night of Broken Glass), and in 1989, the East German authorities opened the wall that had divided the city for twenty-eight years.

Chapter Seven

To Berlin: Meeting Albert Speer

'Avoid married women; they'll blow you further than gunpowder will fire you.'

John Profumo, Minister for War.
Commissioning parade, Aldershot, 1961

On 23 May 1945, two weeks after the surrender of German forces, British troops arrived at Glücksburg Castle, near the German border with Denmark. They were to arrest Speer along with other members of the Flensburg Government; this brought Nazi Germany to a formal end and the beginning of the Nuremberg War Crimes trials. With the arrest of the Flensburg Government, the German High Command also ceased to exist.

At the 1946 Nuremberg War Crimes trials in southern Germany, Professor Albert Speer, then Hitler's right-hand man, also his personal architect, and then armaments minister for the Third Reich, was sentenced by the Allied judges to twenty years' imprisonment in Berlin's bleak and notorious Spandau Prison. He was sentenced along with six other top Nazis convicted of war crimes against humanity, crimes stemming from their responsible positions within the Nazi Party, which directly ordered mass war crimes against humanity. Unlike the majority of their fellow senior Nazis before the court, these seven escaped the death penalty solely because, although highly complicit in the German war effort, it could not be proven that they ever personally, directly or indirectly, ordered or took part in the deaths or crimes of anyone.

Following the fall of Berlin and the defeat of Germany in 1945, Berlin had been divided into four Allied sectors, with the French in the north, the British centrally and the Americans to the south; within these three sectors, everyone enjoyed free movement. The Russian sector, the largest of the four, theoretically further divided the city into two halves, east and west. In August 1961, at the height of the 'Cold War', and with East-West relationships precarious and rapidly deteriorating, Russian tanks could be seen assembling along the communist side of the Berlin Wall, seriously alarming West Berliners, and the western Allies.

For many years I have lectured on the subject of guarding Spandau Prison, the holocaust, and the rise of Nazism in Germany; these are overlapping subjects which have continued to interest me for a number of curious reasons. Firstly, I was born in 1943, during the Second World War and I came into this world, unlike my contemporaries, who were born despite the leaders of Nazi Germany waging war against Britain, but directly because of one of them, Adolf Hitler's deputy, Rudolf Hess. One year earlier, at about 6.00 pm on the night of 10 May 1941, Hess made an unauthorised solo flight from Augsburg in southern Germany in a prototype long-range Messerschmitt 110. As well as being Hitler's deputy, Hess was an accomplished sport aviator and test pilot. He was completely familiar with Luftwaffe military protocol and had access to all necessary aviation material such as maps, radio direction beacons, and flight paths. He was also a good friend of Willy Messerschmitt, the designer of many of Hitler's Second World War fighter planes. This friendship gave Hess unlimited access to the latest military aircraft. Hess had persuaded his friend Messerschmitt to install long-range fuel tanks into the new Me 110 fighter plane, ostensibly for Hess to test the aircraft when fully laden with fuel, but, in reality, it was to enable him to undertake his secret flight to Scotland; it was a misguided mission to persuade Britain to become neutral.

Messerschmitt had no idea his friend was about to undertake such a dangerous and clandestine mission. Hess's plan was to fly to Scotland so that he could meet up with Lord Hamilton, who he had met on a number of official social occasions prior to the war. Hess wrongly believed Lord Hamilton had direct access to the king, and that when he offered Britain peace, the king would accept. Had this plan been successful, Germany would have been in a position to focus its full aggression against Russia. The Hess plan was so obscure that only two close friends knew what he had in mind: the anti-Nazi and former Army General, Professor Karl Haushofer, and his son Albrecht. Later, after the failed 20 July plot to assassinate Hitler, papers were found by the Gestapo, in a conspirator's house, which indicated that Albrecht was implicated in the Hess flight; he was arrested by the SS and taken to the Moabit prison in Berlin where he was interrogated then shot. Professor Haushofer and his wife then committed suicide rather than face a brutal interrogation.

Hess's flight was certainly remarkable, especially being undertaken in complete secrecy and total darkness. In the late afternoon he flew north from Augsburg in southern Germany, then north across Germany and, having successfully evaded a chasing German fighter plane sent to identify the mysterious aircraft, continued north along the Danish then Norwegian coastline until opposite Scotland. He then flew west across the North Sea. Flying below 100 feet, he flew on towards Glasgow to avoid British radar, and then gained altitude in order to safely parachute onto Lord Hamilton's estate, which he identified by its two prominent lakes, leaving his aircraft to crash nearby. Hess injured his ankle on landing. Controversy continues to surround the last minutes of Hess's flight; it is believed two British fighters were scrambled to intercept the flight, but were then called off. Did the British know of the Hess mission, or did they feel one lone German plane was not worth the effort? Official reports are ambiguous.

Hess was swiftly arrested, and over the next few days was interviewed by military and security officials. On instruction from Winston Churchill, the British government totally ignored Hess's proposals for peace, much to Hess's astonishment, and interned him as a prisoner of war for the remainder of the conflict. He was initially sent to the Tower of London and then on to Wales.

As a VIP prisoner, Hess was sent to the secure Maindiff Court Hospital near Abergavenny in Wales. During the approach to Christmas 1942 my parents, Winston and Sylvia, had been married for just one year; my father coincidentally found himself on a short course in Wales. He was a junior officer in the Royal Artillery Regiment and was waiting for a troopship to take him to India; my mother worked as a typist in one of the government ministries in London. For unknown reasons, my father was detailed to be part of an escort that took Hess on an excursion to Surrey, believed by my father to be for medical reasons. That weekend, my parents somehow managed to meet up in London, and nine months later, with my father now in India, I was born at Caversham, near Reading – in the middle of an air raid.

Mother and baby then moved to live with her parents at 62 Hatherley Road, Reading. My earliest memories are of this tiny two bedroom, terraced house in a backstreet of Reading, formally one of an identical number of streets of houses specially built for employees at the nearby Huntley and Palmers biscuit factory. It had a 'front room' which was traditionally never used, a tiny living-come-dining room, a room where my mother washed clothes and, of course, a small kitchen. The toilet was of the 'outside' variety. The garden was very narrow, and I clearly remember playing in the street, often barefoot. Hatherley Road was about one mile from the River Thames, and its banks and inlets were a favourite haunt of mine. From the age of seven I was allowed to go there unaccompanied and it took me about twenty minutes to get to the river and, once past the odorous gasworks, I was in unspoilt countryside. Sometimes I would fish with a homemade rod, but I don't recall catching anything. I had a camp hidden in some scrub overlooking the river and spent many happy hours along the river bank exploring its nooks and crannies. Although a non-swimmer, I did once try bathing but was put off by the soft mud. Being able to be alone along the river gave me access to explore, which I loved.

Aged ten, we moved to a small holding on the outskirts of Eastbourne.

I enjoyed school, but then seriously failed myself by passing the 11 plus examination, and admittance to Eastbourne Grammar School – which I hated. Moving from a class of eight pupils with a kindly lady teacher in a small village school, to a class of thirty disciplined and clever fellow pupils, was tricky. We learned new subjects by rote: Latin, French, physics, chemistry and mathematics, all of which were alien and new to me; life on a farm was incompatible with academia and I struggled.

In the 1950s Eastbourne was a popular town with a sizeable international student population. As a teenager I regularly met with young German students and I was always curious about the reasons behind German enthusiasm for the Second World War, and of the motives of people such as Adolf Hitler, and his top coterie of senior military officers and intellectuals. I knew from school history lessons, and from the typical interest boys then had in matters Nazi, that Germany was traditionally warlike, as well as being one of the most cultured European countries. Aged sixteen, my focus briefly turned from shooting over the marshes surrounding our home to urgently catching up on my neglected studies for the looming GCE 'O' Level examinations.

With the examinations just a few weeks away, I was called to the headmaster's office; Mr Shaw kindly explained that I had the potential to do well in the exams but this depended on my preparedness to undertake some belated study. Because I liked him, and he made good sense, I settled down to study for the remaining four weeks. To everyone's astonishment I passed all my exams with good grades.

Now, just seventeen and fresh out of school, and pondering my future, I found myself and my school friend 'Olly' Oliver visiting the Imperial War

Museum in London. Olly was desperately keen to join the army, but had decided to first complete two years in the school's upper sixth form. While waiting for a bus in London's pouring rain, I noticed an army recruiting poster depicting a soldier standing under a palm tree with the caption 'Come and Join Us'. In a matter of seconds my mind was made up. The following day I reported to the Army Recruiting Office in Brighton, where I was interviewed, without much enquiry on the part of the recruiting sergeant, then medically examined and sworn in as private soldier 23854864 with the Royal Sussex Regiment, to start training on Monday, 6 March 1961 at Wemyss Barracks, the Home Counties Brigade Regimental Training Depot at Canterbury in Kent. My course was due to commence two weeks later, and to my delight and astonishment I was paid two weeks' pay and sent 'on leave'. I was now in the army. I went home and told my parents; my mother was delighted that I was going straight to the army. At this stage I had no idea what an officer was.

I loved the army's basic training and learning the skills of the infantryman, the weapon training, drill and live firing on the nearby Hythe ranges. Every aspect of training was great fun and I revelled in the physical activities of military exercises and training, and I was being well paid instead of relying on pocket money. Having the required five GCE passes, I was soon whisked off for officer training at Mons Barracks in Aldershot, which then trained national service and short term Commissioned officers.

Officer training was all-encompassing and ranged from learning how to fire various weapons, mastering military skills including practical leadership and understanding the complications of leading a team of thirty soldiers, some of whom would have years of service and who had certainly seen military action. Such thorough training was essential to prepare junior army officers to function under the most pressing conditions, such as how to maintain morale in extenuating situations, lead exhausted soldiers to their objectives, and then successfully complete the mission. The training system was hard but effective; it had stood the test of time and still works remarkably well with friendly countries around the world sending their best army cadets, together with young members of their royal families, to Sandhurst. The strictest of inspections were carried out daily, rifles had to be spotless, kit needed to gleam, lockers had to be kept neat and tidy, and there was always the risk of one's locker being overturned if something was not quite right for the inspecting sergeant. Spending all one's time with like-minded people taught us social skills, and prepared the cadets for life in a busy officers' mess; the *esprit de corps* was vital. Any non-cooperation on the part of a cadet meant instant removal from the course, and being served with the dreaded 'Return to Unit (RTU) Notice'.

With just four weeks of the course remaining, the possibility of actually becoming commissioned was now becoming more of a reality, and cadets faced having to choose which branch of the army might suit them. My choice was the Welch Regiment, the 41st Infantry Regiment of the Line; they were a rugby-playing regiment and were just commencing a three year posting to West Berlin, the heavily garrisoned city 100 miles behind the iron curtain then dividing Europe. I was delighted to be accepted by General Coleman, the Colonel of the Regiment.

The offer was conditional on successful completion of the officer training course, which included the final and much-feared 'battle camp' held in the vastness of the very hilly Brecon Beacons. This was an arduous exercise, in patrol groups of six officer cadets, with command of each patrol changing each day. It was the ultimate test before the all-important commissioning parade. The exercise, traditionally held in driving Welsh rain, was a live firing, continuous seven day-and-night marathon of attacks, defences, and forced route marches. There were rigid deadlines to reach the next checkpoint to receive the next orders, and some food. We all understood that late or non-arrival of the group at a checkpoint within the allocated time was to be avoided at all cost, and usually involved the person responsible being re-coursed; this encouraged strong cohesion within the group. Accidents and incidents of exhaustion were inevitable, and withdrawal from the exercise involved being re-coursed to undertake the following full six-month course. This happened to one of my friends, who, exhausted on completing the exercise, fell while climbing into the back of a truck and broke his leg. He was taken to Brecon Hospital by one of the staff and, en route and in great pain, was informed he would be re-coursed. My group accomplished all the tasks and we reported back, totally exhausted, and within the time limit. With battle camp successfully completed, we lucky survivors were trucked back to Aldershot, with just one week to prepare for the final commissioning parade. By now the course numbers had fallen from 200 to just over the required 100.

Then disaster struck.

It was Tuesday morning and we were in the middle of a rehearsal for Saturday's commissioning parade when we were all brought to a halt by the regimental sergeant major, and to my horror my name was called out. I was doubled (ran) to the adjutant's office. Fearing the worst was about to come, I breathlessly stood to attention until the Adjutant looked up and a short question and answer exchange followed.

'How old are you?'

'Eighteen, Sir.'

'When were you eighteen?'

'Last month, Sir.'

'You're too young. How did you get through the officer selection process?'

'No one asked my age, Sir.'

At that point the assistant adjutant interrupted us for the adjutant to take an urgent telephone call from the War Office. I could overhear parts of the conversation and it was clear the international situation surrounding Berlin was seriously deteriorating. The War Office then instructed the adjutant that all officer cadets listed for commissioning and due to join units in Germany, especially the three newly commissioned officers going to Berlin, were to go directly to their postings following the commissioning parade. This fortuitous call meant me staying on the course, much to my great relief. I quietly thanked President Khrushchev of Russia for flexing his military muscle, although my commissioning leave disappeared. My parents and brothers attended the commissioning parade; the inspecting officer was John Profumo, Minister for War, who in his lunchtime address to the cadets advised them to 'avoid married women as they'll blow you further than gunpowder will fire you.'[1] He was soon to be dismissed from government for dallying with Christine Keeler, the mistress of the Russian military attaché in London. Following the parade, and with the parents' commissioning lunch behind us, it was back home to pack and then make my way to Gatwick for my flight to Hannover, and then onwards by the British military train to West Berlin to be based at Brooke Barracks. I remember being in some apprehension of the journey, never having flown or been abroad before, but armed with military passes and tickets I felt reasonably in control.

After the flight to Hannover, I was taken to join the British military train to Berlin. This five-carriage train travelled daily between Berlin and Hannover, carrying British military personnel travelling to or returning from leave, but mainly to maintain the arrangement formally agreed between the four powers, for 'freedom of access' by rail. The train had to stop each way at Helmstedt in East Germany, where the officer in charge of the train presented the passenger manifest to the duty Russian officer. I soon learned that it was customary for the two officers to exchange token gifts; the Russians craved Zippo lighters which could be purchased in West Berlin for a few pence, but were unavailable to the Russians, who would usually present a small bottle of foul-tasting vodka. The journey through the Russian Zone took three hours, and on arrival in Berlin I was met by the regiment's duty officer and taken to Brooke Barracks.

I was given a good-sized room, fully equipped, directly overlooking Spandau Prison, home to the remaining three Nazi war criminals, Rudolf Hess, Hitler's deputy; Baldur von Schirach, Hitler Youth leader; and Albert Speer, Reich armaments minister. The following morning I presented myself to my commanding officer, Lieutenant Colonel Stevenson, and then, accompanied by the adjutant, I was introduced to my thirty-strong platoon, mostly young national servicemen from the Welsh valleys. Within the hour, along with my fellow officers, we were rushed to the officers' mess to be briefed by Colonel 'Steve', fresh back from an emergency conference at the nearby British headquarters as there was a disturbing and deteriorating political situation developing with the Russians.

Prior to the building of the Berlin Wall, the regular duties of any junior infantry officer stationed in Berlin focused on keeping one's soldiers occupied, fit and ready to undertake whatever was required of them, usually ceremonial occasions. Until then, my platoon and NCOs had been spending their collective time on exercises in the nearby Grunewald Forest, undertaking occasional border patrols, and rehearsing ceremonial parades. Then, at midnight on 14 August, everything changed for the British and their French and American Allies serving in Berlin. Under the pretext of protecting its border, the East German government ordered the construction of the infamous Berlin Wall, and a secondary barbed wire border around West Berlin; this took everyone, civil and military, completely by surprise. Suddenly West Berlin was totally closed off from East Berlin and East Germany and locked in 100 miles behind the Iron Curtain. The British garrison and our French and American Allies were given orders to commence a sustained 24 hour peace-keeping task of counter-patrolling in armoured vehicles and jeeps around the East German border. It was especially exciting for someone just out of school and now commanding a platoon of soldiers with instructions to observe the large numbers of Russian and East German troops and police massing along the border of the British sector of West Berlin.

By November 1961, Berlin was in mild turmoil, especially militarily and politically. I commenced my duties in this political 'hot spot' just as Berlin was being divided from the rest of Germany, on orders from the suspicious and unfriendly Russian and East German authorities. For the occupying powers, and Berlin's citizens, there was a hub of apprehension mixed with excitement; the rapid construction of the wall through the city, and barbed wire border with East Germany, were nearing their completion, and Berliners were still in a state of shock and suffering fearful apprehension as to what might happen next. Most West Berliners had relatives in East Berlin, and were now denied any access to them, personally or by telephone. Berlin was in turmoil; the apprehension caused by the sudden construction of the wall, and new barbed wire border around the outskirts of Berlin with East Germany, were nearing their completion. Berliners on both sides of the new border were all in a state of shock and concern for what might happen next.

The regiment's officers were instructed to prepare for a new 24-hour regime of patrolling the 3-mile British section of the 28-mile-long wall being constructed along the 'north to south' boundary through the centre of Berlin, shortly to be known to the world as the 'Berlin Wall'. We were also to commence patrolling along the 20-mile barbed wire outer border between the British Zone and East Germany. In preparation for our new patrolling roles, the regiment's officers were given a rapid tour of the city area and the Berlin Wall in a fleet of army jeeps. I thought that, compared with London, the centre of West Berlin looked comparatively modern, while the residential areas appeared to consist mainly of modern but stark tower blocks, about five or so storeys high. The streets seemed unusually wide, but there were few vehicles; a thriving and cheap tram system covered the whole city.

The communist East German authorities, seemingly subservient and pro-Russian, surrounded outer West Berlin with a heavily guarded 87-mile-long, 12-foot-high, barbed wire barrier, interspersed with guard posts every 100 yards, and constantly patrolled by a heavy East German military presence, complete with fierce-looking dogs. This new reinforced border was intended to halt the increasing flow of East German civilians seeking refuge in West Berlin. At the same time, the East Germans rapidly completed the infamous 8-foot-high Berlin Wall, which was 28-miles long and completely shut off all civilian access between East and West Berlin. In a matter of days a 200-yard 'death strip' of anti-personnel mines was laid along the whole length of the communist side of both the barbed wire barrier around West Berlin, and the heavily-guarded wall, thereby forcibly preventing East Berliners from even approaching the outer border or wall. Watch posts were erected within sight of each other, and armed East German soldiers constantly patrolled with

Albert Speer with mistress Eva Braun, Hitler's future wife. (*Public domain*)

The newly-appointed Speer with Hitler. (*Bundesarchiv*)

Hitler in 1930. Hess is beneath the flag and Goering is to Hitler's right. (*Public domain and from Hitler's Mein Kampf*)

1933. Hitler takes control, with Hindenburg and Goering. (*Debling collection*)

Hitler and Röhm, 1933. (*Debling collection*)

Hotel Lederer am See (former Kurheim Hanselbauer) in Bad Wiessee before its demolition in 2017. (*Teilzeittroll via Wikimedia Commons*)

Passers-by 'encouraged' by SA to read the SA newspaper, *Der Stürmer*. Slogan, 'With the Stürmer, against the Jews'. (*Debling collection*)

A typical 'rounding up' of Jews. (*Courtesy Berlin Holocaust Museum*)

Reichstag before the fire. From Hitler's *Mein Kampf*, 1925.

The Reichstag ruin post-war. (*Public domain*)

1923 banknote – ten million marks. (*AWG*)

Rescuing Mussolini. The Storch and precarious downhill take-off slope. (*Public domain*)

A young Speer with Hitler and Hess. (*Public domain*)

Speer with Hitler. (*Public domain*)

Speer driving a prototype tank. (Signal *magazine, 1943*)

The only known photograph of Speer at a concentration camp. (*Courtesy Berlin Holocaust Museum*)

The infamous 'selection ramp' at Birkenau concentration camp. On arrival: 'Right to work, left to die'. (*Courtesy Berlin Holocaust Museum*)

Albert Speer (left), Karl Dönitz and Alfred Jodl (right) after their arrest by the British Army in Flensburg, May 1945. (*Public domain*)

Defendants on trial. (*Courtesy Berlin Holocaust Museum by Raymond D'Addario*)

Albert Speer. The 1946 Nuremburg Trial commences. (*Debling collection*)

Spandau Prison. The main entrance. (*Public domain*)

Spandau Prison. The main cell corridor. The prisoners' cells were on the left side. (*Public domain*)

Remains of
Hess' plane.
(*Public domain*)

The British
military
train. (*Welch
Regiment
archive*)

YOU ARE NOW
LEAVING
BRITISH SECTOR

East meets West. A
border crossing point
for allies only. (*Welch
Regiment archive*)

Author at the Brandenburg Gate, 1961; Reichstag in background. (*AWG*)

Eva Braun in playful pose. (*Debling collection*)

The Allied division of Berlin and outer perimeter. (*Courtesy Berlin Holocaust Museum*)

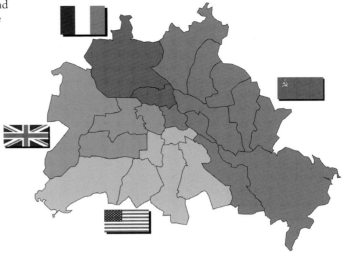

Russian War Memorial at Brandenburg Gate. (*Adobe Stock*)

Christmas Duty at Brandenburg Gate, 1961. (*AWG*)

CAUTION! You are <u>now</u> leaving WEST BERLIN. (*Welch Regiment archive*)

East German workers
building the wall.
(*LIC-22601-P6Z3Q1*)

Scene of the incident. (*AWG*)

Daily Mail, 10 March 1962.

Rejected

It was also revealed today that
Marshal Koniev has replied to
the Birtish Army protest about
the shooting of Cpl. Douglas
Day, driver of a British Military Mission car.

I understand Marshal Koniev
has rejected every point made.

British headquarters have also
hushed up another border incident, which occurred 19 days
ago.

A young Army lieutenant and his
driver on border patrol in the
Eiskeller Enclave were taken
prisoner at gunpoint by East
German police and detained
for three hours.

British policy is not to make the
situation worse by taking
reprisals for pinpricks. But it
is earning a reputation of
appeasing

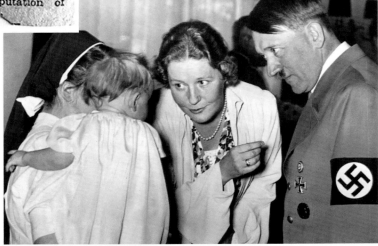

Eva Braun with Hitler.
(*Public domain*)

Geli Raubel, Hitler's niece. (*Public domain*)

A card from Baden-Powell. (*Source unknown*)

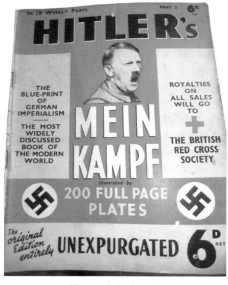

Mein Kampf, Hitler, Adolf. 18 July 1925. Note
- Royalties go to the British Red Cross.L

Author at 'Checkpoint Charlie', 1962. (*Welch Regiment archive*)

Author at 'Checkpoint Charlie',
1998. (*AWG*)

orders to shoot would-be-escapers. Divided and desperate Berlin families could only wave to each other from a safe distance.

To remove any ambiguity as to their seriousness, the East German government then issued shooting orders (*Schießbefehl*) to their border guards to further deter defectors. These orders described people attempting to cross the wall or border as anti-state criminals who needed to be shot. One instruction reads: 'Do not hesitate to use your firearm, not even when the border is breached in the company of women and children, which is a tactic the traitors have often used.'[2]

Nevertheless, many attempted to escape to the West, and did so successfully, but a few were unsuccessful, shot under a hail of bullets as they ran for the boundary line with West Berlin; a number of these attempts and consequences were witnessed by this author. Allied forces were under strict orders not to assist or intervene in such escapes. During the years of the Berlin Wall, around 5,000 people successfully defected to West Berlin, some using the most ingenious means. The number of people who died trying to cross the wall is estimated to be well above 200; the number killed trying to cross the outer boundary around West Berlin is unknown.

Shortly after my arrival in Berlin, and having been thrown in at the proverbial 'deep end' with constant patrolling duties, I was 'pinged' to undertake my first duty as guard commander in charge of the thirty soldiers manning the outer prison wall of Spandau Prison. This dark and gloomy prison housed the last three Nazi criminals, Rudolf Hess, Hitler's deputy; Baldur von Schirach, the Hitler Youth leader; and Albert Speer, Hitler's architect and armaments minister. This duty was considered 'boring' by my fellow officers, but to me it held the prospect of considerable excitement. I knew of my father's connection with Rudolf Hess, and I was excited by the prospect of meeting Hess and reporting back to my family. I had read about the three Nazi prisoners therein, and over the following two years I would regularly volunteer to 'fill in' when vacancies occurred in the rota so that I could learn more. To me, it was an interesting release from the constant monotony of border patrols dominating our duties at this period. It was during my first Spandau duty that I came face-to-face with the three prisoners. All had been sentenced to long terms of imprisonment following their respective convictions for Second World War war crimes at the Nuremberg War Crimes Trials in 1946. Schirach and Speer would not be released until 1966, Hess would die in Spandau.

At lunchtimes, and according to prison protocol, the military guard commander was invited to lunch with the governors and senior staff in the prison officers' mess. Lunch was a formal affair with meals served by waiters; the guard commander was invited to sit with the hosting governor. It was during my first prison lunch that I tentatively expressed a wish to briefly see Rudolf Hess. My request provoked curiosity from the British governor; I explained that Hess was directly responsible for my very existence, and the explanation amused him. I asked if I might even say something to Hess, which I had wanted to do since I first knew that I would be able to undertake the role of prison guard commander. At the governor's cautious suggestion, we surreptitiously lingered sipping coffee until the other governors had departed the dining room; he then took me into the inner prison, where the duty warder was about to release the three prisoners from their cells for their afternoon exercise in the garden.

Due to the sequence of coincidences that brought me to Berlin, this first visit into the inner prison would be where my acquaintance with Albert Speer would begin. Little did I know the occasion would be the beginning of a most unusual friendship between us.[3]

Thereafter, I would seize any opportunities of volunteering for extra duties as guard commander at Spandau, normally an unpopular duty, as this gave me extra opportunities for my unofficial conversations with Speer, the one Nazi leader who was prepared to talk to me. I made notes of our conversations; these are the subject of Chapter 8. It was, after all, a remarkable opportunity for someone, whose peer-group friends were still at school, to speak with Hitler's former friend, most senior advisor, and respected confidant, and who rose to become the second most important Nazi after Hitler. I immediately appreciated that my opportunity for meetings with Speer would be highly unusual, and presented me with a unique opportunity not to be missed. To conform to the complicated prison rules surrounding the prisoners, permission to talk with Speer first had to be obtained from the British prison governor. Very discreetly, unofficial permission was granted, except during any period when Russian officials might be passing through; this enabled me to spend many hours chatting with Speer in the prison garden; we covered many topics, and he was usually happy to discuss his own experiences during his tumultuous years of association with Hitler.

Initially, Speer was not impressed with me having joined the army aged just seventeen, and teasingly opined at our first meeting that I should still be at school. Nevertheless, he took a shine to me, and over the following two years I learned much from him about his own rise to power, his attitude to Hitler's top people, and of his own appointment as Hitler's architect before he became the Third Reich's armaments minister during the Second World War.[4] At one of our early meetings, Speer commented that his first meeting with Hitler mirrored my first meeting with him. Hitler was the Führer when Speer first met him as a freshly qualified but otherwise insignificant architect. We were now one rung down on a similar ladder; Speer, latterly the most senior Nazi, was now talking to an insignificant young British army officer. Speer and I soon established an excellent rapport, and each benefited from the other's company – perhaps because his own family visits were infrequent and officially restricted to less than an hour under strict supervision, and with no physical contact with relatives.

Our conversations were always private and took place in the prison garden; they were informal personal chats, in both English and German, and formed part of my 'continuing education', as Speer described our meetings. He was very keen on improving my linguistic skills, which, under his guidance, progressed at a remarkable pace. In 1963 he was especially pleased when I passed the Civil Service German interpreters' examination at my first attempt. Sitting in the prison garden, he always spoke freely and answered my questions without the possibility of him gaining any benefit except fleeting company. For my part, my questions were unobtrusive as I did not wish to upset or provoke him, and, equally, his answers were plausible and rarely evasive. After all, he was locked up in a dark place, and even visits from his family were rare and short. I believe he simply enjoyed the opportunity of freely talking with a young person without any implications for his answers. Of course, he was also able to tease out of me snippets of national and international news, he was very keen to think that he was still up-to-date with world affairs. Today, as a retired clinical psychologist, and with the benefit of some hindsight, I can better understand his early motives for seeking high office. In 1961 and aged eighteen, I had negligible knowledge of adult life, or the deeper ramifications of recent history – and I certainly knew nothing about psychology, childhood moulding, human motivation, greed or fear for one's life, all of which I later realised had affected Speer as an intelligent young person growing up and developing under the dictatorship that was Nazi Germany.

I knew from school history lessons that, after defeat in 1918, Germany was impoverished as a result of the punishing and draconian post-war Treaty of Versailles, which effectively demolished German industry and extracted reparations beyond the defeated country's ability to pay. Like every young German growing up in this era of extreme austerity, Speer's diaries admitted that, as a young person, he was swept along by the bludgeoning Nazi system that not only offered employment, but controlled the country's media, press, schools, academia – in fact, everything. Due to much good luck, his academic brilliance and skill, the young architect Speer soon found himself on Hitler's payroll in Berlin, which was just as well as he needed to earn a living; before 1933 there was little work for young architects, and he was recently married.

During our various conversations, Speer did his best to hide from me any knowledge he might have had of the nationwide brutality of Hitler's official bullies, the SA, SS and the Gestapo.[5] Or later, of the fate of German Jews and those peoples whose neighbouring countries had been so savagely overrun by the German military, usually rounded up at gunpoint, and forcibly transported to Germany to work as forced labourers. These workers frequently toiled in inhuman conditions across most of Germany's pre- and wartime commercial areas; they were forced to work in factory production, general manual work, agriculture, and anywhere manpower was in short supply. Dissenters were liable to be beaten, shot out of hand, or sent to a concentration camp. Speer always maintained that the Jews working in factories under his control were better accommodated and fed than those in concentration camps; his rationale was that meeting targets depended largely on having a healthy workforce. When asked about the infamous underground factories built by his organisation at Mittelbau-Dora, next to Buchenwald concentration camp, he appeared to go blank. He commented that underground factories were not within his sphere of knowledge, and he could not comment other than to say he was never consulted about such camps.

Speer frequently reminded me that to have argued, challenged or opposed Hitler's orders, he would have risked arrest, along with his family and work colleagues – and likely execution. Not an easy seat to occupy when those in high places knew that in 1934 Hitler had ordered and personally participated in the murder of his own best friend, Ernst Röhm, and several hundred of Röhm's senior staff, who died with him in front of SS firing squads.

Following his eventual release from Spandau in 1966, some authors believed Speer was able to keep the enormous fortune he amassed during his association with Hitler.[6] Indeed, he had long been one of the highest paid of the very top Third Reich officials, and over nearly ten years he skimmed vast sums, through his architectural consultancies, from arranging lucrative contracts for Hitler's numerous building projects. But I found no evidence of such post-war wealth, only hardship for his family. Any personal wealth had long since been rendered worthless by the inflation which had destroyed the currency at the war's end, or confiscated by the Allies; his family was permitted to retain the family house Speer had earlier inherited from his father, where his wife and children lived during his twenty years in Spandau. During this period, the Speer family's need for an income, even just for food, was taken care of by Rudolf Wolters, a fellow architect and long-standing friend of Speer, who organised the means to meet their financial needs. Speer always knew that, on his eventual release, his only way back to financial independence would be through writing his biography, which he did very successfully.[7]

Over the two-year period of our meetings, there was much that took me by surprise, which included Speer making an admission of his long-standing relationship with Eva Braun, allegedly Hitler's mistress, and just days before her death in Hitler's bunker, Hitler's wife. Speer had got to know Eva over a period of some ten years, and Eva, certainly vivacious and pretty in her younger days, often accompanied the trusted Speer family on their holidays, at the request of Hitler, to give Eva 'a break'. This was much to the annoyance of Frau Speer, who was well aware that her husband spent many long weekends at Hitler's mountain retreat at Berchtesgaden in the Bavarian Alps, often in the sole company of Eva. While Hitler was otherwise engaged with his generals, inevitably into the early hours, it was a standing instruction from Hitler that Speer was to look after Eva; both were civilians, neither was permitted to attend these closed 'Führer meetings'. Hitler knew full well that Eva had already tried to commit suicide on at least two occasions, citing boredom as the cause, and Hitler did not want her left alone for long periods. In 1932 she had shot herself in the chest, and then, in 1935, she overdosed on pills.[8] Speer would, in Hitler's opinion, have been a safe companion for her.

In early 1964, my posting in Berlin came to an end when the Welch Regiment was posted to the School of Infantry at Warminster in Wiltshire. For reasons that eluded me, my posting was to the Armoured Vehicle Demonstration Troop, the most sought-after appointment among my peers. I remained in this post until the autumn of 1964, when my army short-service commission expired. The attraction of staying in the army had now waned; being engaged to a Berlin girl was problematical as the army was still sniffy about German wives. I was also getting bored with the unsubtle taunts from the regiment's newly-appointed commanding officer that I was a 'grammar school' officer, as opposed to having been to public school or privately educated. My departure took place a few months prior to my twenty-first birthday, which coincided with an unforgettable mess party and the presentation of two silver goblets from my colleagues. The following morning, I set off in my ancient 'beetle' to tour Europe en route to Berlin to marry my fiancée. Everything was positive. Europe beckoned, and a well-paid civilian position as an interpreter in Hannover was waiting.

My accounts of meetings and conversations with Speer were naively recorded in an old, but treasured, schoolbook. Most of these details have remained unseen; although, over the last twenty-five years, I have given numerous lectures to schools and groups on the subject of 'Guarding Spandau Prison'. My presentations, brief and shallow given the restricted time allocated for a presentation, emphasized the personalities of the three prisoners I had met during my service in Berlin, namely Rudolf Hess, Baldur von Schirach and Albert Speer. In time, this lecture proved the most popular from my lecturing repertoire.

While serving in Berlin I developed a form of grudging respect, and even an understanding of Speer, although I always remembered he was a convicted war criminal. I always addressed him as 'Herr Speer'; I was his *'Englische Leutnant'*, Speer's usual greeting at our meetings.

Chapter Eight

Berlin

'The most dangerous place on earth.'
President J.F. Kennedy, 1961.

By July 1945, the Russians had already occupied all of Berlin before they handed the other three sectors to the Americans, British and French (later collectively known as West Berlin). The British sector of West Berlin was then occupied by the Berlin Infantry Brigade, a garrison independent of the British troops stationed in West Germany, known as the British Army of the Rhine. The Berlin Infantry Brigade consisted of some 3,100 men in three infantry battalions, an armoured squadron, and a number of support units. This occupation lasted until the unification of Germany in 1990. The French Army also had units in Berlin, the *Forces Françaises à Berlin*, and the US Army's unit in Berlin was the Berlin Brigade.

Berlin now found itself isolated by being 100 miles behind the Iron Curtain in the middle of communist East Germany. In effect, the city became a West German island, surrounded by the Soviet Zone of occupation, with the Western Allies occupying and administering the three western sectors of the city. The Western Allies were each guaranteed an air corridor to their individual sectors of Berlin, and the Soviets also informally allowed road and rail access between West Berlin and West Germany. But tension remained high between the Western Allies and Russia, which gave rise to the post-war period becoming known as the 'cold war'.

West Berlin was now surrounded by Russian and East German military. While on regular border patrols, it was nevertheless easy for me to see that Berlin was a stunning city. Compared with London the city centre looked modern, while the outlying residential areas appeared to consist mainly of new tower blocks five or so storeys high; there were fewer cars to be seen, but a thriving and cheap tram system spread across the city. As I loved maps, it was easy to understand the layout of the city; the British section of the Berlin Wall went right through the centre of the city, which was dotted with famous landmarks including Charlottenburg Castle, Potsdamer Platz (Place), the Gedächtniskirche (Memorial church left untouched since bombed in 1944) on the Kürfurstendamm, the Brandenburg Gate, the Reichstag, the Russian War Memorial (and tank with, reputedly, the bodies of the tank crew still inside), and the Reichstag, or the remains thereof, which once housed the heart of the Nazi government.

When not on patrol, guard duty at Spandau Prison or exercises, life in the barracks was taken up with sport, drill and lectures. For the officers, the officers' mess was a comfortable haven of normality, with excellent food prepared by our ever cheerful German chef, Günter. With Christmas 1961 approaching, the few junior officers and soldiers were offered the opportunity of spending Christmas Day with a German family. Numerous local families had participated in a scheme to 'adopt' a single soldier for Christmas. Always being ready for a new experience, I accepted the offer and was promptly invited to meet my allocated family in advance. I arrived at their home, a small flat, to meet them, a very German mother with a son older than me and two daughters. The head of the family had been a Colonel during the war but was lost in Luxembourg in the war's final phase. The youngest daughter was still at school and the same age as me; she took an immediate shine to me, so Christmas 1961 was a cheery time especially as my platoon was 'pinged' for the Brandenburg Gate duty during the week leading up to Christmas. This was a hectic week, as the West Berlin media reminded Berliners that their safety that Christmas depended on the Allied soldiers thus keeping them away from their own families. The result was predictable; the West Berliners turned up at the Brandenburg Gate in their droves with Christmas gifts for the soldiers. Such was their generosity that instructions were necessary to gather in these gifts for onward distribution to every soldier in the regiment, not just for those at the 'sharp end'.

The conversation in the officers' mess was dominated by the communist action, and no one knew how the situation would resolve itself. Since the East Germans had shut all access to West Berlin, the British army was tasked with constant patrolling of the outer border around Berlin, with two additional full-time static duties, each occupying one whole platoon; there was the Icekeller, a small one-farm enclave belonging to West Berlin, but situated one mile inside East Germany, the other was at the Brandenburg Gate, monitoring 4 miles of the wall between the French and American sectors. The Brandenburg Gate was the most interesting, overlooking the Berlin Wall and next to the still-ruined Reichstag building. Both were the focus for the world's visiting politicians, celebrities and press. To facilitate this important and highly visible British border duty, the West Berlin authorities swiftly erected several temporary pre-fabricated wooden buildings as accommodation and feeding stations, and another as a command post. These were built immediately behind the Russian War Memorial at the Brandenburg Gate. They were rather luxurious, with camp beds, wonderful showers, tables and chairs, a rest room with a television and a fully-equipped kitchen, although our meals were all delivered hot and ready from the regiment's kitchens at Brooke Barracks, about 12 miles away, on the other side of Berlin. When on patrol, the soldiers were always 'on guard' as it was known the East Germans would shoot would-be escapers. During the regiment's deployment in Berlin, at least 200 people were killed or died in other ways directly connected to the East German border. Some thirty people from both East and West, who were not trying to flee, were shot or died in border incidents. This included eight East German border guards who were variously killed on duty by escaping deserters, fellow border guards, fugitives, some helping fugitives, or a West Berlin police officer. Around the whole West Berlin border, another estimated 250 fleeing East Germans died. There was no legal requirement for the East German guards to shoot to kill, but the reality of their indoctrination was that guards who shot and killed escaping fugitives received adulation, commendations and bonuses.

Christmas morning was the traditional occasion when the regiment's officers were invited to the sergeants' mess for pre-lunch drinks. Being the youngest officer, I was their unwitting target for intoxication, and due to my naivety, they soon succeeded. I seemed to remember, somehow, taking a taxi to the German family for their early evening celebrations, although I was rather the worse for wear and arrived an hour late, they forgave me. In 1964 I would become engaged to the youngest daughter upon finally leaving Berlin.

Berlin fascinated me. First documented in the thirteenth century at the crossing point of two important historic trade routes, Berlin is 7 per cent water, with a network of eighty or so lakes through which the rivers Havel and Spree flow. Half of Berlin is covered with parks, forests, fields, rivers, lakes and canals with about 30 beaches and nearly 1,000 bridges.

Since the mid-seventeenth century, when its population stood at 100,000, Berlin was popular with many outstanding thinkers, including the philosophers Georg Wilhelm Friedrich Hegel, Karl Marx and Friedrich Schleiermacher. Conversely, and ever prone to civil unrest, the city underwent its first popular uprising in 1830, when tailors' apprentices took to the streets over working conditions. The Revolution of 1848 again led to a bloody clash between soldiers and the civil population. By this time the city's population had risen to 415,000 and in 1871 Otto von Bismarck, the prime minister of Prussia, united Germany, with Berlin the capital of the German Empire. The Prussian Empire of 1871 was history. At this time the population of Berlin had grown to 850,000. The population has continued to grow through to the present time to 3.5 million, with Austrian, Dutch, French, Jewish, Polish, Russian and Turkish immigrants contributing to the population mix.

Allied aerial bombing during the Second World War destroyed the previously vibrant city and took the lives of an estimated 52,000 civilians. Another 100,000 of them died in the ferocious Battle of Berlin, launched by the Soviet army on 16 April 1945. During the war's five years of bombing, nearly 70,000 tons of bombs fell on Berlin, which devastated the city. The net result was the virtual destruction of inner Berlin, which was made worse by the damage caused by the brutal Russian bombardment and assault on the city. The Russians then deliberately humiliated the survivors by encouraging the uncontrolled mass rape of the city's women while embarking on an orgy of looting German homes of everything that could be stolen. Factories were then stripped of their machinery; estates were divided up and allocated to the homeless and peasant farmers. Young German youths who appeared to be between the ages of 15 and 18 were rounded up by the Russian secret police, the NKVD, to prevent even a hint of resistance; they were either removed to forced labour camps or sentenced to harsh imprisonment. The Russians had learned well how modern invading armies could behave, having themselves suffered from the appalling excesses and cruelty of the invading German Army; Russian losses were estimated at 25 million fatalities, including 15 million civilians, so it was no surprise the Russians reacted with savage revenge against the German population. Within days the Russians commenced the arrest and purge of surviving anti-communists, most never to be seen again. Berlin was effectively destroyed; it is estimated that for every citizen of West Berlin, there was 30 cubic metres of rubble that was dumped within the western boundary when it was decided to build a rubble hill over the former Nazi military-technical college, the (*Wehrtechnische Fakultät*). This man-made feature was given the name 'Teufelsberg' (Devil's Hill) after the nearby Teufelssee (Devil's Lake), and rises some 300 feet above the surrounding Teltow plateau in the north of Berlin's Grunewald

Forest. During the Cold War, the hilltop was a specially built US listening station to monitor Russian communications.

After the Second World War, Germany, as it existed in 1937, was reduced by most of the former eastern German territory, with the remainder divided into four military zones of occupation, namely American, British, French, and Russian, all under the authority and conditions of the post-war Yalta and Potsdam agreements. At the same time, Austria, and its capital Vienna, were jointly occupied by the Allies, mainly to prevent Russia seizing Austria; the country remained divided until 1955.

As the economic recovery in West Germany significantly outperformed the Russian Zone, the communist government in the East enforced tight control over its borders, especially as more than 100,000 East Germans and East Berliners fled to the West annually. In June 1948 the Russians tried to cut off the Allied sectors of West Berlin by blocking the rail, road, and canal access with West Germany. The Allies responded by initiating the Berlin Airlift, which took place between June 1948 and May 1949. During the airlift Allied aircraft carried approximately 2.3 million tons of cargo, mainly food and even coal, at a cost to the West in excess of 200 million US dollars.

East Germany finally closed its borders between East and West Germany in 1952. The intention was to isolate West Berlin and slow East German migration to the west, but, because of the quadripartite Allied status of the city, the 29-mile-long sector border between East and West Berlin remained open. As there was still freedom of movement between West Berlin and West Germany, East Germans could still access West Berlin and then fly to West Germany.

In 1961 Western relationships with the Russians deteriorated further, due in part to the increasing flood of defections to the West via West Berlin, especially by East German academics and professionals. These people fled due to miserable working conditions prevailing across East Germany, and they were generally suffering from long-term depression, having lived under the Third Reich and now under the puppet East Germany on the orders of the oppressive Russians. The East German secret service, the *Stasi*, operated a massive and successful denunciation policy, taken over from the former Gestapo, employing 200,000 officials to sift reports from those willing to denounce family members or work colleagues. Prospective escapers were aware that getting caught would result in lengthy prison sentences; all East Germans knew that citizens successfully fleeing to the West would be officially recognised as refugees, and receive relocation assistance and state financial benefits. By now nearly three out of 18 million East Germans had crossed to the West. Then, on 13 August 1961, an East German water-cannon truck was symbolically deployed against West Berliners protesting in front of the Brandenburg Gate, and at midnight on 14 August, under the pretext that Western demonstrations necessitated their intervention, the East Germans commenced construction of the infamous Berlin Wall, taking everyone, civil and military, by complete surprise. West Berlin was effectively closed off from East Berlin, both physically and ideologically. All East Berlin streets, hundreds of bridges, paths, windows, doors, gates and even sewers opening to West Berlin were systematically sealed off by walls, concrete block barriers, barbed wire and metal gates. A 200-yard zone behind the wall was cleared, mined and guarded by the Soviet-controlled East German authorities, who then militarised the entire border of East Germany with the West, a formidable undertaking. Under the Four Power Agreement post Second World War, access to East Berlin was still available to the three military powers via the American 'Checkpoint Charlie', a well-guarded Berlin Wall crossing point.

Within days, the East Germans had cut Berlin off from West Germany by building a substantial wall right across the city from north to south; it was 12-feet high and approximately 27 miles long and was followed by a barbed wire border around the whole of outer West Berlin with East Germany. This border barrier was a further 70 miles long and was protected with 300 guard towers, foot patrols, an estimated 1 million anti-personnel land mines and around 3,000 attack dogs. Machine-gun posts and searchlights were sited at likely escape points. Day and night, the East German *Volkspolizei*, the *Vopo*, patrolled their side of the Berlin Wall and along the outer Berlin border; telephone lines between the East and West were cut. Letters could be written, but all mail was subject to *Stasi* censorship.

The Allies were perplexed; the border barrier around West Berlin was now heavily manned, guarded and controlled by the East German military acting on Russian orders. Access routes across the Russian Zone to West Germany were strictly monitored by the *Vopo* to prevent contact between citizens of East and West Germany and Berlin. The immediate Allied response in Berlin was to initiate regular and intense patrolling along the whole East Berlin border, both across and around the city, by their respective military personnel.

West Berlin was effectively an island, cut off from West Germany although still accessible to the Allies by air, along with one highly-guarded rail line and a strictly controlled pot-holed motorway in poor condition. The combination of Western and Berliners' defiance had already ensured West Berlin had become symbolically significant as an 'island of peace and freedom' during the Cold War; its people would need to remain resolute and defiant. To ensure its survival, West Berlin was already heavily subsidised by West Germany as a showcase of the West, and its people prospered in stark contrast to the drab, almost lifeless and car-less militarised East Berlin, with its Moscow-like, characterless, gloomy housing blocks.

The month of October 1962 brought with it considerable excitement, and some real fear. Earlier, in May, America suspected the Russians were secretly building missile sites on Fidel Castro's Cuba, right on America's doorstep and just 90 miles from the USA mainland. This was intended by the Russians to be in retaliation for America having placed nuclear missiles in Turkey, aimed at Russia. Apart from seeking to level the balance of power between Russia and America, putting missiles on the island of Cuba was also a Russian attempt to dislodge the Allies from Berlin, which had long been a painful thorn in the Russian side. By September, US spy planes had successfully photographed the secret construction of a number of Russian missile silos across Cuba. American diplomats protested bitterly at the United Nations, and faced with a potential escalating military crisis, President Kennedy ordered the interception of an approaching Russian convoy of missile-carrying ships bound for Cuba. On the Cuban Atlantic approach, American warships formed a line beyond which the Russian ships would not be permitted to sail. Two days before the confrontation, and with international tension escalating to previously unknown levels, President Khrushchev of Russia put additional and serious pressure on the Western Allies by moving Russian tanks into East Berlin and positioning them at strategic locations along the wall. The theory in the officers' mess was that Berlin was now in the crosshairs of every Russian gun and missile, and that the Russians could bounce Berlin as easily as a tennis ball. And they were correct; any retaliatory military action by America would have certainly resulted in the Russian military swiftly overrunning Berlin.

Within two days of a potentially serious confrontation between Russia and America, the regiment was placed on the highest alert; weapons were issued and sleeping in combat uniform was the order of the day, with vehicles ready to rush the 12 miles to assist colleagues already patrolling the wall. As the tension rose, it was clear to all that the Russian fleet was still following orders to proceed. No one knew what either the American warships or the Russian convoy would do when they met. The regiment and all Allied troops in West Berlin were allocated defensive positions; my platoon was despatched to guard a block of some fifty flats of frightened West Berliners overlooking the Berlin Wall. Within no time at all, a number of Russian tanks arrived and positioned themselves in a single file with the leading tank just 20 yards from us across the wall, its barrel aimed straight at 'our' block of flats. The German civilians in the flats were seriously frightened, but had nowhere else to go. Similar columns of tanks could be seen arriving all along the wall and it was clear there would be little we could do to stop them. Had the order been given, they could have just driven through the wall. My thirty soldiers were each armed with an SLR (self-loading rifle), and I seem to remember being given a pistol and a box of grenades. No orders came, either to defend the flats, fight to the end or surrender if overwhelmed. If the event had not been so serious it would have been funny. We borrowed a transistor radio from one of the flats' residents and listened to the constant news bulletins as the Russian ships approached the American warships. I believe most of my soldiers thought their end had come.

Then, on 25 October, and with just hours to go, and to everyone's obvious relief, Khrushchev gave the order for the Russian ships to about-turn. We all cheered, and our German hosts, who had all been quietly but fearfully waiting in their rooms watching news programmes, suddenly appeared with lots of cakes, wine and crates of beer. We had a merry few hours with our hosts before being collected for the return to barracks. Only then did we hear that the Cubans had meanwhile shot down an American military aircraft and opened fire on others. The Russians swiftly put a stop to such incidents. However, early on 27 October, an American aircraft dropped a number of harmless 'signal' depth charges near an uncontactable Russian submarine still lurking in the Cuba approach, the *B-59*. The intention was to get the vessel's captain to respond to messages instructing it to withdraw. The captain, Valentine Savitsky, misunderstood the American action and, thinking he was at war, prepared to launch one of his nuclear missiles at an American target. Fortunately, one of the three officers with the missile launch code, Vasili Arkhipov, guessed the sounds were signals and demurred. He refused to insert his launch code thereby stopping the action. He was later decorated by the Russian authorities for his calm action. At the next regimental dinner in the officers' mess, we all drank to the health of Vasili Arkhipov, for being the man who saved the world; in reality he probably did.

On 27 October, following hectic diplomatic negotiations, the Cuba Crisis was peacefully concluded. The world breathed a sigh of relief and my platoon settled back into the routine of border patrols and occasional guard duties at the prison. On 26 June 1963, President Kennedy visited West Berlin and gave a public address known for its famous phrase '*Ich bin ein Berliner*'. It was popularly taken to imply that Kennedy was claiming to be a citizen of Berlin; having been present, I can verify this section of Kennedy's statement. When he made his speech he actually said:

> Two thousand years ago, the proudest boast was 'civis romanus sum' (I am a Roman citizen). Today, in the world of freedom, the proudest boast is 'Ich bin ein Berliner'! All free men, wherever they may live, are citizens of Berlin, and therefore, as a free man, I take pride in the words 'Ich bin ein Berliner'.

Having been the focus of the world during the crisis, West Berlin was the city to visit; it appeared wealthy and vibrant, and it was famous for its distinctly cosmopolitan character, and as a centre of education, research and culture. On 3 October 1990, the day Germany was officially reunified, East and West Berlin formally reunited as the city of Berlin. Today it is the capital and largest city in Germany by both area and population, and the second most populous city of the European Union after London.

Chapter Nine

Spandau Interviews with Speer

'A creeping evil which took us all over'
Speer on Hitler.

This chapter is based on the author's written notes made at the time of the interviews with Albert Speer in Spandau Prison. The annual international prison rota for Spandau Prison 1946–1987:

Britain: January, May and September
France: February, June and October.
Russia: March, July and November.
America: April, August and December.

4 January 1962

Meeting Rudolf Hess, Baldur von Schirach and Albert Speer
On the day of my first prison duty visit I was excited at the prospect of such an unusual task and hopeful of getting sight of these three prisoners – all famous men. The January day was freezing cold and even by midday when my platoon began assembling for the short march to the prison it was still icy grey and snowing. On the snow-covered parade ground of Berlin's Brooke Barracks my sergeant had formed up the guard ready for inspection. We were all wrapped up in our dark green, very warm winter warfare suits, which was just as well as the temperature was –20°C below freezing. The army had just issued revolutionary new waterproof and rubberised comfortable boots, which soon earned the nickname 'cobbly wobbly'. They were especially good in icy conditions, as we were about to discover. Ammunition was issued; the prison relief squad was cursorily inspected by the adjutant before he retreated from the biting cold and trudged back to the warmth of his office. We then trudged off, it was too slippery to march, all of us slipping and sliding along the icy cobbled road under the watchful eye of my platoon sergeant; we led a squad of three corporals and thirty soldiers from the barracks to Spandau

Prison, a journey of just 300 yards. On arrival we were admitted into the inner courtyard where the previous guard from my regiment had paraded ready for the handover. Presented with an army revolver and holster, I was informed it had to be worn at all times. With the short handover process completed, my sergeant posted the guards; there was a small degree of luxury for the duty guard commander: a dingy room that had a bed, desk and chair. The general consensus of my colleagues was that the task was boring, so, on advice, my overnight bag contained a book and writing paper.

My first task was to familiarise myself with the layout of the outer prison wall, with its guard towers protecting the inner sanctum holding the prisoners. The day-to-day running of this inner area, which included the prison cells and administrative offices, was the responsibility of the civilian duty governor and their staff. The four governors were always in residence, whereas the guards' presence coincided only with their own nation's monthly tour of duty. The towers around the perimeter wall were within sight and hailing distance of each other, and overlooked the garden into which the prisoners were allowed twice each day. The towers, known to the soldiers as 'goon boxes', were stark and unheated. They all had an interior glass box for shelter, and an outer level from which both the inner garden area and exterior of the prison could be observed. Even though the outer level was exposed to the elements, these walkways always smelled vaguely of urine. The British soldiers joked that the cabbage-like smell was definitely Russian; soldiers were not expected to need such facilities during their short two-hour stint on guard.

I admit that entering the inner prison came as something of a shock and reminded me of childhood visits to descend the damp and slippery spiral staircase into the dark dungeon at Pevensey Castle. Spandau was cold, dark, gloomy and heavily foreboding like a prison scene from a scary Dickens novel. Because of the number of cells available in the prisoners' corridor, an empty cell was left vacant between each prisoner's cell; this was originally to avoid the possibility of prisoners being able to communicate with each other, a rule later relaxed after they were permitted to meet up each day in the prison garden. The remaining cells in the wing were either left empty or designated for the prison library, while another became the prison chapel. The individual cells were approximately 10 feet long by 9 feet wide and 12 feet high; each was equipped with an iron bedstead with sheets and blankets, and a rough wooden table and chair was provided together with a small shelf. Each cell had a flush toilet in the corner, which smelled strongly of disinfectant. The cells were spartan but clean. Cleaners were not employed; the prisoners were required to undertake a daily cell and corridor cleaning ritual, partly to remove the paint flakes from the peeling walls and ceiling. My impression was that this cleaning ritual, rigidly enforced, was to remind the prisoners of their lowly status.

My overall sensation was almost an out-of-body experience; it was as if I was not really there, but somewhere back in time. Everything I was seeing appeared remote and unreal, I was also fully aware the occasion would be unique, I was about to see some of the most infamous leaders of the Second World War.

Standing alongside the British governor, I watched the duty warder getting ready to unlock the three prisoners. It was a short walk from their bleak, individual cells to the extensive prison garden for their afternoon of 'free time'. All aspects of the garden, and the prisoners' activities, were under the watchful eyes of my soldiers manning the observation posts atop the outer prison wall. At the appointed time, about 2.00 pm, the senior warder opened each of the three cell doors and stood back. Slowly, the three prisoners, dressed in ill-fitting prison uniforms, emerged and stood motionless in front of their respective cells; there was no eye contact with the warders. Their movements were slow and methodical, like a drill movement, but in slow-motion. On noticing the governor, there was a perceptible shuffle, which I presumed was akin to standing to attention. The governor nodded to me, I stepped forward and quietly introduced myself to Rudolf Hess and, in a short sentence, in my inadequate school German, uttered the sentence that started my relationship with Albert Speer: *'Herr Hess, Ohne Ihren friedenssuchenden Flug nach Schottland wäre ich nicht geboren worden, so danke.'* ('Herr Hess, without your peace-seeking flight to Scotland, I would not have been born, so thank you.')

Clearly taken by surprise, Hess completely ignored me, pulling a face as he sloped off. Schirach, a half-American German, also ignored me and strode away. Their response nonplussed me but Speer brought me back to my senses when he turned to me and, in perfect English, casually asked me to clarify my ambiguous comment. Unsure of prison protocol I stepped back but the governor accompanying me indicated with a wave of his hand that I could speak to Speer, who then invited me to join him in the snow-covered prison garden. I followed him through into the garden where he indicated a bench, we both sat down and he asked me to explain my statement to Hess. I related that, in 1942, while Hess was a prisoner following his failed mission to Britain, my junior officer father had once escorted Hess on one of his trips from Wales to Surrey, believed by my father for medical reasons. This duty enabled my recently married father, who was about to be posted to India, and my mother, who was then working as a secretary at the War Office, to meet up in London before my father joined his ship the following Monday. I was born nine months later. Speer was amused by this explanation, he teased that I should still be in school and we chatted for a while.

During my first meeting with Speer, I could see Speer was intrigued by my Hess account, especially as the tale unfurled in my truly awful school German. Flitting between English and German, we chatted for an hour or so, during which time he appeared to be building an image of who I was and my personality. He asked questions about my schooling, my home town, and my reasons for joining the army. He was especially keen to know what was happening across Berlin. Without newspapers or a radio, he was not privy to the latest news about the East-West stand-off; he had heard snippets from the warders and was clearly perplexed. I briefly explained that the East Germans had built a wall dividing East and West Berlin and then surrounded the city with an impenetrable barbed wire border. He merely nodded; I presumed my comments were just confirming what he had already overheard from the warders talking. As this particular conversation drew to a close, we were getting cold, Speer made me a surprising offer that I could not refuse: if during my forthcoming visits I wanted to properly learn German, he would teach me 'Hoch Deutsch', which I understood to be 'correct' German. I naturally accepted, and over the following two years, under his excellent tutorage during my irregular guard duties at the prison, I progressively mastered the language and went on to become an interpreter. Speer was always completely relaxed with me, and came over as a perfect older-generation gentleman; of course, he spoke excellent English, with a typical German accent, but I formed the impression his interest was primarily to perfect my German.

10 January 1962

Having just completed several bitterly cold days on border patrol, a couple of free days in the warm and comfortable officers' mess was going to be most welcome, especially as it was snowing hard. My plans for a relaxing day were short lived; the Adjutant requested someone to voluntarily undertake an extra Spandau duty for an unwell colleague. Regimental tradition held that officers were not ordered, they were requested. With the prison duty offering the opportunity to again speak with Speer, I volunteered. Within the hour my prison relief was struggling through the deep snow towards Spandau. The wind felt particularly icy as we trudged along in our heavy but warm winter apparel. The prison looked even more dark and foreboding. Inside the inner prison compound it was just as cold; out in the 'goon boxes' it was even colder, as they caught the brunt of the icy wind. Once the first guards were posted, I read through the instructions, and finding nothing to the contrary, suggested to my sergeant that we change the guard every hour, not every two. I was keen not to have soldiers frozen at their posts. The system was inconvenient for the NCOs responsible for changing the guards, but they agreed; the change worked well and no one complained.

Following lunch, and with permission from the British governor to speak with Speer, we met again in the garden. Due to persistent driving sleet, we sheltered in a small shed in the garden. We chatted for about an hour, but then we both agreed that we were getting too cold. It was a pity; Hess and Schirach had decided to remain in their cells, which meant that Speer and I could talk freely. Hess had a tendency to complain if anything unusual occurred, such as someone talking to his fellow prisoners, though he seemed to ignore me, perhaps because I was in uniform. In that hour, Speer dramatically improved my understanding of the German language; he gave me a quick guide on how to master German verbs, which included a reasonably simple method of rapidly learning the language by using one of four possible word endings (the *me*, *you*, *we* and *us* of conversation). At school, this was called 'verb conjugation', and the complicated method of its teaching at Eastbourne Grammar school had successfully confused me. As Speer pointed out, his was a simple method of understanding how to adapt a verb in a sentence and consequently speak good German, and without too much effort. His advice unlocked one of the unfathomable complexities of the German language, which had formerly baffled me, and set me off to learn as many useful verbs as I could; he suggested about 100 would be enough to become familiar with the system. During our subsequent meetings, he was always quick to give me useful hints relating to sentence structure and pronunciation. This transformed my confidence, as until that point, I had embarrassingly relied on my rather basic 'schoolboy' German. Early on in our discussions, and with the benefit of observing him at close range, I never once perceived Speer's character as being 'typically' German; he was always confident, quiet, dignified and kindly.

We changed tack to discussing how he was coping with life in prison, especially having once held such a high position with all the rewards of that office. He replied by saying that he was now paying the penalty for having served Hitler; to Speer it appeared to be a logical consequence. He stated he had followed Hitler as his personal architect, and due to his ability, he had been taken into Hitler's inner circle. He went on to say that if it was a crime to have become a minister under Hitler, then he was guilty and would serve his sentence without complaint. There was a pause before he added that he was never involved in any war crimes, and that he spent his working life avoiding politics to concentrate on his architecture, and later on, he assumed responsibility for food supply, transport, and during the war, armaments production.

I asked him how it was possible that Hitler took him, as a young man, into his tight circle of advisors and ministers. Speer thought that Hitler appeared to recognise himself in his (Speer's) quiet and knowledgeable personality as an architect, something Hitler craved but never achieved. He added that Hitler appeared mesmerised by his architectural planning, to the extent that Hitler would invariably just glance at Speer's plans and nod his approval, as if he, Hitler, had prepared them himself. When I asked about his affluent lifestyle as a minister, he replied in his quiet unassuming manner that, in this respect, he was like Hitler, never ostentatious, and that he had never engaged in stealing from Europe's museums or banks. He admitted to having been aware of other Nazi leaders' overt greed for stolen property, but maintained he had never participated in such grand theft. He did point out that as the minister in charge of various departments, he had once realized it was necessary to initiate a policy of banning his officials from accepting or demanding bribes from contractors, on pain of punishment. This was clearly an area that Speer was confident to discuss with me; indeed, I noted that he was almost animated when talking about his innocence, to the extent that he added that the war crimes judges had agreed with him, hence his relatively lenient sentence. He brought our conversation to a close with the comment that he fully understood it was necessary for the Allies to convict him, due to his close association with Hitler. With that comment, we both got to our feet and walked back to the inner door, and a few degrees of welcome warmth.

In between the incessant border patrols, I did manage to visit my new German family for the occasional meal and to 'chat up' the young Dorothea. Their company and hospitality made life much more pleasing, and it was a hectic, happy time until a minor misfortune occurred. With East-West tension still high, each side continued to maintain their individual 'right of access' to the others' sectors. On the morning of 6 March 1962 a Russian staff car with two officers and a driver was legitimately in West Berlin when it was involved in a traffic accident. Under the four power agreement, Allied troop incidents could only be dealt with by other Allied officials, not by civilian police. On this occasion, the West Berlin police incorrectly detained the Russians to begin their own investigation. News of their arrest quickly reached official Russian circles in East Berlin. Meanwhile, I was on border patrol duty with my driver in a remote area in north East Berlin, known as the 'Eiskeller', when we suddenly came up against a group of a dozen East Berlin police, the Volkspolizei or *Vopos* as we called them. They had come through the barbed wire border near one of their 'goon boxes' and were positioned across our track through the forest. Naturally we stopped and were quickly surrounded by the *Vopos*, with submachine guns being pointed in our direction. *'Raus Raus'* was the shouted order, clearly meaning 'get out' of the vehicle, which we did. Not wishing to over-excite an already jumpy cluster of twitchy *Vopos*, I told my driver, Private Bendall, to comply but to stick with me.

Due to the heightened tension along the border, our pre-patrol briefing had included a reminder of the necessity of caution. Just one week earlier Corporal Douglas Day had been shot while driving an official British Military Mission car. This had resulted in a formal British protest to the Russians. With our hands in the air, we were both taken at gunpoint through the border fence and then ordered into the back of a truck. I then knew what it was like to be taken as a prisoner of war, but without the war. We were then driven off, leaving our abandoned jeep. I knew our abduction would soon be discovered as the standard ten minute 'all's well' coded call would not be made; nevertheless being arrested at gunpoint was a scary experience, especially as it was getting dark.

Under the armed guard of *Vopos*, we were driven for about twenty minutes before arriving at a barracks on the outskirts of Staaken, an East German town near the border with West Berlin. Taken into one of the barrack rooms, we were met by several older men wearing the ubiquitous black leather jackets of plain-clothes *Vopos*. Their presence waiting for us was a strong indication that our abduction had been planned. We were independently but politely questioned about regimental strengths and the purpose of the constant Allied patrolling; but it was only a few weeks earlier at Mons that my intake of officer cadets had been instructed how to behave in the unlikely event of any one of us being detained anywhere in the world. And here I was, detained by communist soldiers. And so I answered as instructed with my name, rank and number. After a few cups of coffee, the three *Vopo* officers then appeared to give up. I was left with a young *Vopo* officer and tried hard to engage him in conversation; I failed; so we both sat there for a few more hours before his colleagues returned and took us in their car to the nearby Staaken border crossing point with West Berlin. On arrival, our weapons were returned to us; we were saluted and then left to walk across the 200 yards of 'no-man's land' back into West Berlin. Our arrival at the police post was much to the surprise of the West Berlin police on border duty, who were completely unaware of the day's events. On reflection, it was just like a scene from a menacing cold war film – dark, icy and full of threat. A few telephone calls were made and within minutes a British staff car swept up to the border crossing point and we were whisked off to the British HQ for debriefing. There I learned that my experience was believed to be related to the earlier traffic incident with the Russians, and then, after a welcome meal, we were returned to Brooke Barracks where my fellow officers were keen to know what happened. A few gin and tonics never tasted better, and that was that.

19 January 1962
Although it was bitterly cold, Speer wanted to go into the garden as there was no one else about. We took refuge from the cold in a garden shed and chatted about the coming New Year and my progress with learning German. Being curious to know how he thought he would cope, and what he might do, I asked him about his eventual release, although he still had four years to serve. I was also curious to know what he thought about Germany's reaction to him being released, and then I sat back to give him time to think. His immediate response made complete sense to me; he already had a family house in Mannheim and plans were afoot to convert one of the cellar rooms into a facsimile of his prison cell. His fear was that, if he found it difficult to re-adjust after twenty years, it might help if he could retreat to the familiarity of 'his cell'. He was also hoping to see his family more frequently during the final phase of his sentence, hopefully to make his return home less of a shock to them. He had no worries about his neighbours, or local reactions to his return hometown, being sufficiently confident that the press would, en masse, sweep him along in a whirl of favourable publicity.

He was unshakeably convinced the press would make him an immediate and popular 'personality'. His confidence rather surprised me, but I could see his point. Back in 1946 he had successfully convinced the judges at Nuremberg that he was a 'good German', whose only crime was to have been swept along by Hitler into a responsible and powerful position. In our conversations, he was always adamant that he was innocent of any crime against humanity and that, having served his sentence, he should either be ignored or treated respectfully. Due to his fame, or infamy, he was certainly going to be seen as a celebrity. After all, since his trial he was famous across Germany as Hitler's confidant who knew nothing, and Speer acknowledged, from secret approaches by the press, that the German media would be desperate to have an account of his wartime activities and time in prison.

As he was in a positive mood, the question of his ignorance of war crimes naturally came to the fore; was it feasible, I asked, that the German people would believe it possible to have great power, but without having any real knowledge or responsibility for any of the many terrible events? Speer had already given me the impression that he had a rehearsed answer for every major question, and he was happy with his account that he was a civilian architect and only later became the minister of production and armaments, but never a participant in any military planning or war crimes. He pointed out that, throughout the war, Admiral Dönitz had personally ordered the sinking of civilian ships on a wide scale, but was given a short prison sentence because he was 'obeying orders'. He added that, dissention would have been problematic; even during the years before the war, Hitler had ordered the execution of several of his own previously loyal friends, such as Ernst Röhm, a decorated former German army captain and chief organizer of Hitler's Storm Troopers. SS documents reveal Röhm had openly queried some of Hitler's orders, so Hitler made an example of him; Hitler had Röhm and some 200 of his senior officers murdered in what became known as the 'Night of the Long Knives'. Everyone working for Hitler knew exactly how far they could go. During the war years, Hitler exerted full control and demanded total loyalty from his staff and senior officers to the extent that, as Führer, he had over eighty of his generals executed for treason, so no one dared to disobey or challenge Hitler's orders, unless they had a death wish for themselves, their family and friends. Speer was adamant that he had never intentionally caused anyone pain or distress; his standpoint was always that his role was one of supporting Hitler, and in order to be supportive he had to be loyal. Speer was, I believe, being mischievous when he added that he had even been loyal to his slave labour workforce, by ensuring they were cared for and fed. He said he knew bad things were happening, but they were not his responsibility; he claimed to have avoided anything bad, and by not looking he did not see anything, so could not be held directly accountable.

He then made an observation that carried a convincing ring of truth: 'It was not possible for anyone to challenge Himmler or Goebbels – they were Hitler's orders and I was just Hitler's architect – what could I do? I kept my hands clean.'

At this point I felt comfortable enough to ask him if he had read Hitler's book *Mein Kampf*. His first response was 'No', but he went on to say that he had probably been given a copy, but, to him, it was anyway unreadable, and rambled incoherently about German politics and Hitler's aims in a nonsensical way. I commented by asking him about the book's reference to the Jews. He replied that the book wrote about many things, including the Jews, and it was all nonsense, adding that *Mein Kampf* had been written a long time ago when Hitler was in prison; therefore, it was not surprising that Hitler was angry and muddled. Speer reminded me that *Mein Kampf* was not considered by any of the judges as relevant at Nuremberg, and that when Speer came on the scene the book had all but been forgotten.[1] As we rose to our feet, my final comment that day was that Speer followed Hitler to the bitter end regardless of the warnings in *Mein Kampf*. This brought the stiff response from Speer: 'The book was not important. I never read it. I was focused on my career.' To me, he was relying on his earlier trial answers, and anyway, during his years with Hitler, Speer was probably concentrating on matters more important, mostly furthering his own career, rather than reading a book written by Hitler some ten years earlier.

His final comment was that he would not be seeing me for a while as the Russians were about to commence their month's responsibility for the prison. Speer pulled a face when I commented, 'lots of cabbage', knowing the prisoners and Russian guards were fed on the Russians' typical national diet, which always involved cabbage. I wished him good luck.

6 May 1962

It was nice to go back to Spandau Prison. It was now early May and spring was well advanced. Everyone was pleased the 'Russian winter', as we called it, was behind us. Speer was pleased to see me and we took up our previous position on the fragile bench; he immediately wanted to know what was happening beyond the prison walls. There was, in reality, little to tell him, but I did amuse him by relating my experience being taken prisoner by the dreaded *Vopos*, to which he amusingly commented that I now also knew what it was like to be a prisoner. To ease my way into our conversation, I told him I had recently been to the site of the Reich Chancellery and Hitler's bunker, both of which he had designed, both now lay in ruins. He merely shrugged his shoulders, which I interpreted as indifference.

I had already decided on several questions to ask him, and my first related to his trial. After the relaxed conditions at 'Camp Dustbin',[2] did he think he had been well treated and given a fair trial? He said that being accused with the other Nazi leaders at Nuremberg, all charged with serious war crimes, came as a complete shock to him. He had not anticipated being charged as a war criminal; his hopes were of assisting the Allies to rebuild a shattered Germany. Apart from being interviewed at length about Luftwaffe bombing techniques, he was not otherwise consulted. This rebuff brought home to him the realisation that he was in serious trouble; he even had to face the possibility that his life might be at stake. To answer my question, he said the unclean conditions of his detention and bedding left much to be desired with just a straw mattress to sleep on. The food was reasonable, but it was a bad time for him with little exercise to break the monotony. Then he was charged with all four war crimes, but he had a good lawyer (Dr Hans Fläschsner) to guide him in preparation for his trial. The worst moment was after the trial when those sentenced to death were taken from their cells for execution. He commented, 'I don't want to discuss this anymore. Correctly I was found not guilty of the two worst charges but guilty of two others. I have been punished and I have no complaint.' We shook hands and parted.

I would not see Speer again until the middle of May, just before the British handed over their prison responsibilities to the Americans. My life as a regimental subaltern had meanwhile been hectic, with ongoing border patrols, exercises in the Grunewald Forest and, to my pleasure, regular official trips into East Berlin as part of the requirement for the four-power access agreement giving open access to authorised military patrols across Berlin. My colleagues found this duty somewhat boring, whereas I found going behind the Berlin Wall intriguing, so I was able to slot in and take on more than my share of such visits. East Berlin was still showing many signs of its battering from the war, more so than West Berlin, which had mostly been rebuilt and was buzzing with life. Across East Berlin there were large open spaces that had clearly been bombed flat and elsewhere huge piles of rubble dotted the skyline across the city. There were few cars; people travelled by tram or on foot, and they always seemed to be looking down. When we were noticed by locals, they invariably looked away, an indication of the high level of security in their communist police state. We were never approached by any East Berliners. I was fascinated by the number of famous buildings, most were under repair, while others were draped in scaffolding or just standing in a sad and neglected condition. I was intrigued with the Russian War Memorial at Treptower Park, and I would make it a focal visiting point when I took British visitors and our garrison soldiers on familiarisation coach tours of East Berlin. It was a large cemetery, and of great interest to me, and its visitors, was its grandeur; the cemetery and its memorials had all been made of polished marble salvaged by the Russians from Hitler's chancellery building.

On one such duty visit to East Berlin, we were driving along a wide avenue near the Alexanderplatz when we were signalled by *Vopos* to stop. A large well-behaved crowd was gathering so we complied and, out of curiosity, awaited events. A slow procession of large black Russian limousine cars was approaching and people began waving. As the open lead car approached our position, now at walking pace, we could clearly see the escorting convoy was protecting someone important. Then, to our surprise, the lead car came to a halt just beyond us, presumably because our unusual presence had been noticed. Out jumped a plump individual – it was President Nikita Khrushchev himself. He strode over to us beaming a huge smile and shook our hands, then turned back to his limousine and everyone drove off, leaving us rather bemused. Again, in another earlier historical moment, I had escorted the British Prime Minister, Sir Alec Douglas-Home, and Berlin's Mayor, Willy Brandt, later chancellor of Germany, for a private viewing of the Wall. But back to Albert Speer incarcerated in Spandau Prison.

20 May 1962

I returned to prison duty towards the end of May, when Berlin was warm and delightful and the prison garden was filled with flowers in full bloom. After the usual prison lunch, I was again able to meet with Speer as he was being released from his cell. He greeted me warmly and we walked behind Hess and Schirach into the prison garden. We went to the usual bench while the other two prisoners walked off in deep conversation. After a few opening but polite questions about world events and my life in Berlin, I told him of my meeting with Khrushchev and Speer asked if I had any further questions to put to him. One aspect of the war which had always puzzled me was why Germany chose war rather than diplomacy to settle its differences. Speer's response was quick, and, to me, surprising. He reminded me that Germany had not been defeated militarily in the First World War, maintaining with some pride that German troops on the battlefields of France were invincible and could have continued fighting; although Austria-Hungary and the Ottoman Empire were about to announce an armistice with the Allies, the fourth member, Bulgaria, had already surrendered. He then gave me a potted history lesson. The main facts according to Speer were:

On 11 November, the First World War ended followed by the Allies initiating the Versailles Treaty to control and punish Germany. Once the Allied post-war Treaty was announced, it soon brought the remains of the German economy to a virtual standstill, and with the population humiliated and starving, resentment rapidly spread across Germany. In addition to the German navy revolt, soldiers recently fighting in France felt they had been betrayed into surrender by their politicians and harboured great resentment. He reminded me of the effects of the First World War, namely that the Versailles Treaty required Germany to acknowledge responsibility for the war, pay massive reparations for Allied damages, surrender all German colonies outside Europe and worst of all, to severely limit the size of Germany's armed forces. Germany was on its back and no one had any hope. Speer said he believed it was necessary for somebody, or something, to lift Germany out of its crushing poverty and state of national depression. This eventually happened in the form of Hitler, who offered prosperity and a return of German pride. Speer continued by asserting that it was necessary for Hitler to eliminate all political opposition, especially the ferocious opposition of the communists, who would destroy Germany by their allegiance with Russia. When asked about the violent methods used, he merely commented that these people had to be locked up, and if some died, then that was unfortunate. He then commented:

They were violent times; there was fighting in the streets. The communists were very powerful. The people wanted peace. The perpetrators were locked up and that satisfied the people; the police were very popular and the camps were not hidden at all, they were openly discussed in the press.

On reflection Speer continued: 'You must remember that life for the people after the first war was miserable. Here was the nation's saviour. There was work and hope; we had a good life for once. People grew to trust the Nazi party.'

Speer was adamant that it was the failure of politics that led to Germany's plight in 1918, which, in turn, propelled Germany to war again in 1939. This line of discussion neatly led me to ask Speer why Germany had an international reputation for such horrendous violence against innocent civilians. I offered an example: the German invasion of Belgium, Holland and France in the First World War. He remained silent as if he did not understand, or perhaps my question had taken him by surprise. My point was relating to common knowledge that, as early as the First World War, the German army advancing through Belgium and France killed many civilians by the random shelling and bombing of towns and villages, and I added that even nurses were taken from hospitals and shot. Not letting him off the hook, I further commented that Blitzkrieg in the Second World War also involved brutal widespread aggression against civilians. His response was measured and thoughtful, but typical of Speer when asked uncomfortable questions. He replied that Blitzkrieg was the best way to conduct war, as it was quick, but in any war civilians invariably became casualties, and in any event, he was never involved in the conduct of advancing armies; it was nothing to do with him. Being curious about the Nazi consideration of revenge against Germany if they lost the war, I posed a rhetorical question that, if Germany lost the war, and the Allies were invading, did he not expect the Russians to avenge themselves for their earlier suffering, inflicted by the invading German forces? Speer replied, 'We did not expect to suffer defeat, but when it was too late, we slowed the Russian advance to allow many civilians to flee towards the advancing Allies.' But your German cities and people in the east were brutally treated in revenge. Was that not seen as a probability in the event of defeat? Speer replied: 'Yes, that was the penalty for losing the war.'[3] He folded his arms indicating he did not wish to discuss the matter further. I told him I had recently visited Bergen-Belsen concentration camp near Hannover, and asked him if he knew of it. 'No' was his blunt reply. I pointed out that the camp was right next to the village, and local people worked there; what did they think seeing so many dead and dying? Speer replied, 'How can I comment?' A question about the Wannsee Conference elicited the same response, with a mildly sarcastic addendum that he had once owned a house on the Wannsee Lake. A similar question about his possible acquaintance with Reinhard Heydrich elicited an equally sharp negative response.

Having clearly but unintentionally upset him, I decided to press him with one further related question, which was that of the German army's willingness to disregard the safety and lives of Jews, even to the extent of murdering them en masse. Again, his reply came as a surprise as my question about the Jews did not seem to bother him; Speer said that the Jews were not really German, and, being non-Aryans, they did not work and therefore should be encouraged to return to their original countries. He opined that if they would not return voluntarily then they should be forced, and he added that even the English had once brutally evicted its Jews for crimes against the people.[4] The discussion shifted to concentration camps; Speer was adamant that he knew full well of labour camps where foreign workers were housed, but not of concentration or extermination camps for Jews. I noted his comment, he added: 'there was knowing and not knowing, and I did not know.' He again reminded me that he was Hitler's architect and admitted to deliberately avoiding hearing of such things as atrocities and concentration camps. Again, it was a case of not being responsible for, or wishing to comment on matters he knew nothing of. At this point Speer became almost distant, engaging in some involuntary hand twitching. He was clearly embarrassed by this line of discussion, so we switched to talking about the reason for Germany declaring war on so many countries. My point was perhaps naive; I asked him why Hitler felt it necessary to invade so many neighbouring countries when Germany could so easily have dominated Europe with its economic mastery. This seemed to cheer Speer and he readily agreed it was an interesting concept, but not possible while a number of Germany's neighbours retained territory that was originally German, and were suppressing their German speaking populations. I brought the question of *Lebensraum* into the conversation, which earned the response that Germany needed more space for its growing population, and this should be achieved by reclaiming its lost territories and evicting non Germans. Speer was adamant that this could never be achieved by peaceful means, so the military concept of Blitzkrieg, lightning war, was adopted as being the only route possible. Speer added that I should remember that, at this stage, he was employed as Hitler's architect and played no part in Hitler's political or military decision making.

I changed tack by asking if he was affected in any way by Hitler's many speeches. 'Not at all', was the reply. 'I was not interested in the politics of Hitler's speeches.' He said he was, though, interested in how Hitler could mesmerise everyone with his presence and oratorical skill. 'I knew his intention, everyone did, but I was not involved.' I asked him if he ever spoke with his fellow prisoner, von Schirach. His reply was, 'No, he was a 15-year-old schoolboy when he joined the Hitler Youth and never grew up.' I asked him if the same applied to him after he met Hitler. His thoughtful reply was that he, Speer, made an important decision, and thereafter unwittingly moulded himself to conform.

I had seen the 1955 film about the Dam Busters raid on the three Ruhr dams, so to lighten our last few moments of that day, I asked him how he viewed the raid. 'Yes, I was there soon afterwards', was his response. Asked about his impression of the raid he said it was very brave and skilful, but had not really affected German war production. He went on to say that his workers rose to the challenge of repairing the dams by repairing them in just a few months, and he was mystified why his repair operations had not been subjected to follow-up raids. He said such raids would have caused serious problems for his war effort, and wondered why they attacked the Eder dam, which had no part in Ruhr industries, and, in any event, the breach in the Möhne dam was repaired by the several thousand workers he had transferred from the Atlantic Wall to the Möhne and Eder areas. It was all repaired before the winter rains. He smiled when he commented that the biggest problem for Germans living in the area was sewage disposal. Having brought the conversation around to a lighter subject, it was time for this meeting to close.

A few days later I was called to see the regiment's adjutant, Captain Davis, who asked about my conversations with Speer. I explained that the purpose was for Speer to teach me German, and it was soon evident that someone had queried my meetings with Speer during my prison duties as guard commander. Thankfully there was no problem; it seemed our chats had come to the notice of the Russian governor, who queried my motives with his British counterpart, who in turn had mentioned it in conversation to my commanding officer, Colonel Stevenson. I was reminded that the prison was subject to heavy censorship, which I knew, and I gave the assurance that I would have no contact with outside sources or the press. At this point, I was sent on a two week Civil Service interpreter course at Hohne in West Germany, I remember my final examination interview with two unsmiling officials; I was asked about my accent and I could not resist nonchalantly admitting that my tutor was Albert Speer. I was delighted to pass at my first attempt, for which I would thereafter receive a meagre interpreter's allowance. I would not return to Spandau Prison until September, when the British resumed responsibility.

12 September 1962
I had looked forward to my next meeting with Speer to report my language examination success, but on meeting him in the prison garden he was initially rather tense; it appeared that Speer had also been spoken to about our 'German lessons'. Speer believed Hess had made some sarcastic comments to the Russian governor about Speer 'fraternising with the enemy'. Speer told Hess that my father had escorted Hess during his time in England, hence my interest, which seemed to have satisfied Hess. So with the Russian governor not unduly bothered, there was no ongoing problem. Speer was delighted with my new language qualification. It was a fine and warm autumn day, and with Speer now more relaxed, we strolled around the garden and chatted about a few world events before I asked him a question that had arisen since our previous meeting. I was curious to know, if he could have his life again, would he choose the same path that resulted in his conviction for war crimes and a twenty-year sentence, or would he apply his many skills to a successful career in architecture. My guess was that this would be an obvious question for Speer to have pondered, it turned out that he had thought about it many times, but his answer surprised me.

Speer said that he would repeat his experience as Hitler's architect because it brought him to the pinnacle of his profession and to his family came fame, and later, a considerable income. He was adamant that he was not cut out for a steady office-bound career. When asked whether the fame of his association with Hitler was worth being tarnished with Nazi war crimes, he was adamant that they were nothing to do with him, which was a frequent Speer retort to questions about such matters. He then pointed out that, on his release in two years' time, he would again become famous as the 'respectable German' imprisoned for the 'crime' of having been a successful Hitler minister. 'Europe will always be grateful to me', was a comment he made several times during this meeting. It was an interesting aspect of Speer having obtained high and influential rank under Hitler. This conversation led Speer to appear to present the strange concept of himself as a saviour, because, in the final stages of the war, he had undeniably saved Germany from Hitler's 'Nero' order to destroy the nation's commercial and social infrastructure.

Further, he strongly believed he had saved Western Europe by prolonging the war to slow the Russian army's advance across Eastern Europe to Berlin. Speer was convinced that, by him slowing the Russian advance for some ten weeks, he had prevented the Russians from seizing most of Europe before the Western Allies could gain dominance in Central Europe. He made an interesting comment, which I noted, he said 'By now I was the most important man in Germany', so I asked him how this had come about. His reply was that other ministers were too busy with escape plans for themselves and their families, and Hitler was sick and drugged. This was a point that had already been widely raised in the British press and mirrors Speer's later writings.

He added that he had always enjoyed fame, and, to a lesser degree, the accompanying fortune. I understood he now considered himself penniless, and I was curious to know how he thought he would manage financially following his release. This was clearly something Speer had considered, and planned for in some detail during his imprisonment. He explained that he knew full well that he would be offered large sums of money for his unique story, and he was preparing for the anticipated interviews by reading about television, something of which he knew very little. He had already been requested to give a number of such interviews. This discussion took me into new territory, and led me to ask him about his wealth as a Nazi minister, and what had happened to it. He claimed that, after his arrest, he had lost everything of value, along with his bank accounts when his assets were seized by the Allies; this left his family to rely on assistance from his many former friends and colleagues. He claimed to have nothing left with which to support his family, emphasizing that he was never corrupt nor had he ever received plunder. He accepted, though, that he had enjoyed an extravagant lifestyle as a Nazi minister. At that time I accepted his reply; his previous answers had appeared to be honest, and it was years later before I was to learn that, after his arrest, he had admitted to the war crimes investigators that he was a millionaire; what happened to his wealth remains unclear, but all his money and shares would have become valueless by the total devaluation to zero per cent, which totally destroyed the German currency. Speer also kept very quiet about his valuable collection of paintings acquired during his time as a Nazi minister; where, when and how these valuable artefacts came into his possession is unknown outside his close circle of friends. Towards the end of the war, these paintings had been spirited away for safe keeping to Speer's acquaintance, a Dr Robert Frank. After Speer's release in 1966, a number of his paintings were seen to be quietly coming back on to the art market for discreet sale. This aspect of Speer's rehabilitation into society is murky, and the trail of his art sales equally elusive. Even Speer's wife was in the dark about her husband's art collection and sales proceeds; one explanation given by an auction house involved with these discreet sales gave a possible explanation: '*cherchez la femme*'. Events later in London would tend to support this hypothesis.[5]

The regiment's tour of duty in Berlin was entering the final six months of the posting. It was announced that, in November, the regiment would be posted to Warminster in Wiltshire to assume the role of demonstration battalion at the School of Infantry. Accordingly, we would progressively depart from Berlin during the coming months, with an advance party of specialists undergoing training at Warminster in readiness for the new role. My fellow officers were delighted; Berlin had been a 'chore' and not really the traditional soldiering of peacetime parades and socialising. The families and friends of my colleagues were in Wales, and Warminster was not too far away. Talk in the officers' mess swung to the cars they would buy on their return, and the weekend parties that could be attended.

10 January 1963

At our first meeting of the year, it was bitterly cold. Speer and I met in the prison garden, exchanged pleasantries and he bemoaned the freezing cold weather and ongoing strict approach by the Russians. The wind was blasting us; we were huddled in coats and the conditions were not conducive to conversation. I briefly updated him about my posting back to England, and we both acknowledged this year would be our last for such conversations. His response was straightforward, merely commenting that it would be a pity as we had both benefited from our meetings and added that he would have to think of something useful to tell me before I returned to England. The weather conditions were such that we had to break off our meeting and retreat back into the prison.

12 May 1963

For me, this was another regular duty at Spandau Prison. After the bleakness of the previous January meeting, today was a warm summer's day, and after the usual lunch with the governors, I met up with Speer as he was setting off for his afternoon in the prison garden. He was, as usual, pleased to see me. He never knew if or when I would reappear; he knew which month the British would be on duty but not the identity of the guard commander. We went straight to our usual bench and Speer immediately asked me what was new, his usual opening. We discussed a number of world issues, and this led Speer to remind me of his current mission, to walk around the world.

This needs some explanation; at an early point during his imprisonment he decided to walk around the prison garden as many times as was possible each day and recorded the distance. This soon turned into his personal challenge 'to walk around the world' by the time of his release. By 1963, he was theoretically approaching Canada from Alaska and we talked much about his route and what he imagined he saw. He was always animated when discussing his imaginary journey, and it certainly kept him fit in both body and mind.

We moved on to talk about my future plans – and his – he had three years to go before his release. We both decided it was too soon to discuss plans; I certainly had no idea what I would be doing by the time of his release; I guessed he had plans but kept them to himself.

On the grounds he would find something to tell me, I asked if I could make notes and he replied 'feel free'. I still wanted to get into his mind about certain wartime issues and asked him if, towards the end of the war, and with Germany collapsing, what were his feelings, and did he feel any guilt? Again, this was a question for which he appeared to have a prepared answer; he replied, 'No, I had done everything I could; the collapse was not my fault. I was sorry for all the civilians, yes, but it was not my fault – we were all equal now.' I pushed him further and asked about all the invaded civilians? He replied, 'What happened was nothing to do with me.' I kept this aspect to the fore and asked him about its effect on Germany; had it left Germany with a reputation? He replied, 'Without doubt – and we can't win wars either.' He appeared mildly upset by these questions, so I soft peddled by asking him if he felt he would be able to mix with ordinary people on his release. He replied, 'Why not. They will want to know my side, as an architect.'

On being arrested in 1945 at Flensburg, Speer spent an intense two weeks being interviewed by American Air Force bombing experts seeking to assess the efficacy of Allied bombing.[6] I asked why this was of such interest after the event. Speer explained how the Allied mass bombing of German cities and industry, to disrupt the German war effort, had been a total failure. I noted his reply: 'Inconvenient, yes, but we were always able to quickly repair much of the damage, and anyway most of their bombs missed their targets, so the Americans were curious to know why their bombing had failed.' Speer then surprised me, and all became clear when he said:

America was still at war with Japan, and the US Air Force plan was to continue with saturation bombing of Japan to end the war there. I told them it would fail, and that the war with Japan could last for years. They were shocked by my assertion and took my points seriously. I told them, almost as an aside, the only solution for the swift defeat of Japan was to use an atomic bomb.

Speer's answer was, indeed, shocking in its simplicity and implication, and for revealing his cold logic. It appeared to me that Speer saw war as a matter of numbers, nothing to do with people. While making notes, I continued with the question 'So you were responsible for Nagasaki and Hiroshima?' He replied without hesitation,

Indirectly; I pointed them in the only direction possible. At our meetings I proved to them that the conventional bombing of Japan would be ineffective; they had never understood why their massive bombing efforts had not succeeded. All I did was to explain their failure and advise them how to stop the war.

A further thought presented itself, which was to ask Speer if this was why he had received preferable treatment at his trial. Speer replied, 'Of course. Although I was not as important to the Americans as von Braun. He was the future, I was the past, but there was an element of gratitude, I'm sure of that.' (The Americans flew von Braun straight to the USA before the Russians could find him.)

My last straight question of the day was to ask if people might want to know more about his relationship with Hitler. He replied, 'that's irrelevant'. He commented 'enough', and we continued chatting about world events and my return to England. With that he rose to his feet and we both walked back to the door into the prison. We shook hands and he said he was off to walk another few kilometres to get over my questions.

22 May 1963

Today we had a detailed session to consider the intricacies of German grammar. Speer was unusually rather serious, not at all his normal self. He asked me about my plans but this subject would not fly; it fell flat, partly because I had no plans. Speer commented that he did not want to discuss anything about the war, that he was too tired, and having had a cold. We walked a while in the garden but he said little other than to ask about Dorothea, and how she would cope in England. I said that she had already been there and she liked it and that she was looking forward to going. Speer commented that he would like to go to England so I suggested we should meet there after his release. 'Yes, let's meet; yes, that would be good,' was his response. He was now in a better mood, but we had chatted for over a half hour, and he wanted to catch up on his walk as he was behind with his mileage. He bowed his head to me and turned away, so I returned to my official guard room.

25 September 1963

My twentieth birthday. Speer was cheerful and joked that I was still too young to be an army officer, but that he was now getting used to the idea. Being a typical September and autumn in Berlin, the weather was still warm enough to sit in the garden, and Speer was in a good mood. We chatted at length about my return to England, and he was delighted when I informed him that I was getting engaged to Dorothea, the daughter of my adopted German household. By now our conversations were exclusively in German, and he was curious to know how Dorothea and I conversed. The answer was in either language but never mixed up. Dorothea was studying English at Berlin University, so much of our conversation was in English and orientated towards her studies, whereas conversations with her family and friends were always in German. He remarked that my return to the UK was a pity, and we agreed that both of us had benefited from our meetings.

We then turned to some more prepared questions. Knowing I would be leaving Berlin by air, Speer observed that the last time he flew out of Berlin was following his final departure from Hitler, and that he had flown out under Russian artillery fire. He hoped my flight would be less exciting. This comment triggered a question that had puzzled me for some time. I knew Speer held Hitler in high regard even to the end, yet he had told the war crimes judges that in 1944 he had tried to kill Hitler to save Germany from Hitler's order for the total destruction of the country's industry and infrastructure. So, therefore, why did he leave the safety of Flensburg to return to Berlin in such dangerous conditions, when he had already absented himself from Hitler, just three days earlier? (On 20 April.) Speer and his staff knew full well that the Russians had surrounded Berlin, and his staff at Flensburg had been relieved when Speer returned, only to be horrified to learn that, within hours, and for no apparent reason, he intended to undertake the perilous return flight back to Berlin.

I had recently read of this second flight in accounts of Speer's arrest and trial, and to me it was illogical; I asked him why he needed to return so quickly, and in such dangerous conditions. His initial answer was to trace and collect two friends, who would otherwise be killed or captured by the Russians. One was Hitler's doctor in Berlin, Dr Brandt, who had since been arrested by the SS on Himmler's orders; the other was Speer's long-time friend, Friedrich Luschen, the former head of Germany's electrical industry. He was in hiding in Berlin, and fearing arrest by the Russians, had said he would commit suicide, rather than be taken prisoner by the Russians, which he did. Almost as an aside, and in an unusually quiet voice, Speer added that he wished to take his farewell from Eva Braun. This struck me as strange as he had seen her just a few days earlier, so, after some thought, I pushed him further on the point. 'Actually', he said, 'no one knows except me why I went back, not even my adjutant, von Poser.' He went on to say he had never been pressed on this point as enquirers and interrogators logically presumed he had returned to Berlin due to his strong relationship with Hitler. After a pause, he remarked, almost as an aside, that he had gone back to Berlin to try to persuade Eva Braun, Hitler's mistress, to accompany him back to Hamburg to save her from certain death. The following day he flew back to Berlin with that sole intention. There, deep in Hitler's bunker, with the Russians fighting just hundreds of yards away and slowly but determinedly making their way towards the bunker, Speer risked his life for several hours alone with Eva trying to persuade her to leave Berlin. He said he even tried to get her drunk on champagne, but failed to persuade her; she refused to go. At 3.00 am Speer gave up; he absented himself from Eva and made his way back to his waiting Fieseler Storch aircraft and was safely flown back to Hamburg.

We sat in the prison garden for some time without saying anything, until Speer said, 'I left Eva Braun, and now you leave me.' I could see he was upset, an emotion I had not previously seen, and sensed closure was imminent. I asked if talking with me had helped him prepare his account for his prison release. He replied, 'Yes, of course,' and after a pause added, 'it's your generation I have to convince. The older generation will naturally believe me because they need to – there is no such draw for your generation.' He stood up, offered his hand, and said 'Farewell.' With that rather sad but final word, Speer walked back into the inner prison. I never saw Albert Speer again.

With that final admission, I remember being rather lost for words; it explained his motive for his hazardous and final flight to Berlin. I appreciated that I had privileged information, and completed my notes before returning to my room. I thought that, by Speer sharing his secret with someone unlikely to realise its significance, he may have felt this particular ghost had been laid to rest.

On 1 October 1966, Albert Speer, now 61 years of age, and Baldur von Schirach, 59, were both released on the dot of midnight from Spandau Prison, having completed their full sentences of twenty years' imprisonment for war crimes. Due to the insistence of the Russians, not one day of remission was permitted.

Both men were greeted by their waiting families and jostling television crews eager for a story before the ex-prisoners could be driven away from the gathered and over-excited media. Both men appeared oddly dressed, until it was realised they were wearing the same clothes they were wearing when they were sentenced at Nuremberg, twenty years earlier. Speer was driven to the Hotel Gerhus in the nearby Grunewald Forest, where, to calm the thronging press, he gave a short and impromptu press conference in German, English, and French. His initial comment was flashed around the media offices and reads:

> You can see that in spite of 20 years imprisonment, I am in good condition, and since Stalin's death, we have been treated politely and decently. The food was good and sufficient. I say this to contradict some reports that have been spread about the prison.

When asked about his intentions, he replied that he wanted to work again as an architect at home in Heidelberg and to be with his wife, four sons, and two daughters.

Von Schirach, aged 59, was already blind in one eye, and with poor sight in the other. He was divorced in 1959 and went to live with his son in Munich, where a substantial inheritance awaited him from his American mother.

Following his release in 1966, Speer quickly achieved his personal quest for fame and fortune, not as an architect, but as a broadcaster and writer. The underlying theme running through his published works presented him as a high profile victim of Nazism, who was beguiled and duped by Hitler and his coterie of thugs, criminals and psychopaths. It was a theme widely accepted by his audience. Nevertheless, Speer later wrote in his personal diary: 'For there are things for which one is guilty even if one might offer excuses – simply because the scale of the crimes is so overwhelming that by comparison any human excuse pales into insignificance.'

Although a young and impressionable junior Army officer, my memories of Speer remain clear. However, there remains strong suspicion that, like so many who met him, his *Englische Leutnant* was also duped by his charm and personality.

His published works, which perpetuate his claim of innocence, were a phenomenal success, they include:

Erinnerungen (1969)
Inside the Third Reich (Macmillan, 1970)
Spandauer Tagebücher (1975)
Spandau: The Secret Diaries (Collins, 1976)
Der Sklavenstaat (Slave State) (Wiedenfeld, 1981)
Infiltration (1981).

Reflections

When Speer later published his memoires, he was clearly cautious about his second flight to the Hitler bunker in Berlin. On different occasions following his release, he gave two conflicting accounts of this second flight. It was an odd mistake for someone so alert and careful with his choice of words. I believe his conflicting accounts were a smokescreen to hide his long-term relationship with Eva Braun, and by keeping her a secret, his 'good German' reputation remained intact.[7]

In that moment, I could finally understand how his and Eva's relationship developed during the latter years of the war. To comply with Hitler's wishes, Speer had necessarily spent much time at Hitler's mountain retreat, as did Eva. She was highly isolated from human contact, except for Hitler's domestic staff and Albert Speer, and highly vulnerable. Speer had always been an attractive man to women, but he had never publicly even hinted that he might have had a secret side to his life. And so, the father of six children with his wife, Margarete, he was also the confidant and friend of the young Eva Braun. The many hours he spent alone with her gave him ample opportunity to embark on a strong physical relationship with the young woman. And it would have been necessary for the relationship to be a complete secret. Speer knew that enough of Hitler's inner circle were highly jealous of his relationship with Hitler, and they would have been keen to denounce him. Speer knew only too well he was playing a dangerous game by involving himself with Eva; all of Hitler's staff suspected that Geli Raubal, Hitler's 18-year-old niece, and first love, had conducted a number of affairs from Hitler's flat in Munich, one with Hitler's chauffeur, Emil Maurice. On being discovered, the young man was marched away and somehow managed not to be shot. Geli then committed suicide with a chest shot, using Hitler's personal pistol. A number of her friends believed she was already pregnant. On 18 September 1931, a newspaper report of the girl's death appeared in the *Münchener Post* and questioned the veracity of the initial reports:

In a flat on Prinzregentenplatz, a 23-year-old music student, a niece of Hitler's, has shot herself. For two years the girl had been living in a furnished room in a flat on the same floor on which Hitler's flat was situated. What drove the student to kill herself is still unknown. She was Angela (Geli) Raubal, the daughter of Hitler's half-sister. On Friday 18 September there was once again a violent quarrel between Herr Hitler and his niece. What was the reason? The vivacious 23-year-old music student, Geli, wanted to go to Vienna, she wanted to become engaged. Hitler was strongly opposed to this. The two of them had recurrent disagreements about it. After a violent scene, Hitler left his flat on the second floor of 16 Prinzregentenplatz....

Regarding this mysterious affair, informed sources tell us that on Friday, 18 September, Herr Hitler and his niece had yet another fierce quarrel. What was the cause? Geli, a vivacious 23-year-old music student, wanted to go to Vienna, where she intended to become engaged. Hitler was decidedly against this. That is why they were quarrelling repeatedly. On Saturday 19 September it was reported that Fraulein Geli had been found shot in the flat with Hitler's gun in her hand. The dead woman's nose was broken, and there were other serious injuries on the body. From a letter to a female friend living in Vienna, it is clear that Fraulein Geli had the firm intention of going to Vienna. The letter was never posted. The mother of the girl, a half-sister of Herr Hitler, lived in Berchtesgaden; she was summoned to Munich. Gentlemen from the 'Brown House' (Nazi Headquarters) then conferred on what should be published about the motive for the suicide. It was agreed that Geli's death should be explained in terms of frustrated artistic ambitions....

The men in the Brown House then deliberated over what should be announced as the cause of the suicide. They agreed to give the reason for Geli's death as 'unsatisfied artistic achievement'.

But Geli was not alone; in 1937 the well-known German film actress, Renate Muller, also an intimate friend of Hitler, was discovered having secret trysts with a lover and her indiscretions were reported to Hitler. Tipped off that a team of SS officers were en route to arrest and 'dispose' of her, she fully understood the implications and instead chose suicide by jumping from a third floor window rather than face interrogation and death at the hands of the SS. My speculative guess is that Speer's knowledge of all the ramifications of the Geli Raubal and Renate Muller affairs would have added considerably to the excitement of his own liaison with Eva Braun. And one must remember that Eva regularly accompanied the Speers on holiday, always at Hitler's request, but to the annoyance of Frau Speer. Speer had also spent time with Eva in Berlin, where he designed and built her personal apartment at the new Reich Chancellery in Berlin. Of all people, Speer was very aware of Eva's weaknesses, and her need for human kindness; she had twice attempted to commit suicide during her long and unloving relationship with Hitler: the first time (1932), she shot herself in the chest sustaining only a superficial graze, the second time (1935), she allegedly took an overdose of sleeping pills – neither attempt was serious.[8]

Chapter Ten

An Uncertain Conclusion

Initially, post Second World War, it was difficult for the German people to rehabilitate themselves into European society; they had lost the war. By barbarically causing the deaths of many millions, their reputation was shredded, their country was in ruins, and they had a terrible collective guilt complex relating to the war, even though there had been a number of well-planned plots to kill Hitler, starting in 1933. All attempts involved citizens of the German Reich and occurred in Germany. No fewer than forty-two plots have been uncovered by historians. However, the true numbers cannot be accurately determined due to an unknown number of undocumented cases, such as the alleged attempt by Albert Speer himself. The plot which most nearly succeeded was led by Colonel Stauffenberg, a German war hero, with support from a number of senior German generals. The plot, known as Operation Valkyrie, was to kill Hitler with a bomb at a meeting with his senior advisors. The explosion killed and maimed a number of attendees but somehow failed to kill Hitler. The Gestapo immediately initiated *Sippenhaft* and over 1,000 of Stauffenberg's associates and family were arrested; some 600 were swiftly executed.[1] Towards the end of the war, many senior officers realised that the effect of widespread German brutality would create a stigma engulfing all Germans. One such senior officer, Colonel Trescow, predicted the guilt for such widespread atrocities would fall on future generations of Germans. On receiving an order to kill all captured Russian political officers, he angrily observed to trusted colleagues:

> You realise what this means? This will still have effect in hundreds of years, and it will not only be Hitler who is blamed, but rather you, me, your wife and my wife, your children and my children, that woman crossing the street and that boy kicking a ball. Think about it![2]

Indeed, the ruthlessness, brutality, violence and speed of German invasions across Europe had been unprecedented. At the war's close the rest of the world was additionally to reel from a surfeit of horrendous evidence of large scale German inhumanity, which had already been directed against sections of their own population, the sick, disabled, dissidents, undesirables, then the Jews, followed by Russian and East European prisoners of war. This policy of brutality and mass murder was then applied to other subjugated peoples of neighbouring countries. Even for those Germans not directly involved in such brutal behaviour, many had been acquiescent and accepted going into a violent war as a means of solving Germany's problems. German teachers and lecturers had taught Nazi philosophy, police officers had been enthusiastic enforcers of Hitler's laws, with elderly and retired policemen making up the *Einsatzgruppen* (extermination squads), and a good half of all doctors voluntarily joined the Nazi Party, with a significant number to later appear before the special doctors' war commission trial. During 1942, the army had become 'docile participants in genocide'.[3] Many returning German officers and soldiers had participated in, or witnessed, their army and colleagues supervising and performing mass expulsions and executions; it would take a long time psychologically for these individuals to return to normal civilian life, even where they claimed to have been 'obeying orders'.

For all those who survived the concentration camps, including Jews and non-Jews, the end of the war did not bring an end to their problems. Germany was in a state of utter chaos, with its cities, towns and infrastructure severely damaged by Allied bombing; there was mass homelessness and floods of refugees needing food and shelter. Several million terrified Germans from the east had attempted to flee westwards before the advancing Russians; most were overtaken and a combination of the cold, starvation, exhaustion, rape and murder at the hands of the Russians resulted in the deaths of hundreds of thousands of refugees. Speer contributed to many of these deaths by ordering refugees off the roads to prioritise retreating military convoys to continue fighting; German civilians, mainly women and children, were abandoned to their fate. On 15 March 1945 Speer ordered:

> In cases of evacuation, the following sequence is to be applied: Wehrmacht for operational purposes, coal (and) food being cleared out. Even transports of refugees can be taken only after the total fulfilment of these requirements, if empty space that really is unused is available.[4]

The arrival of Allied forces and the collapse of Germany did not bring with it the means to undo the memories and evidence of violence and misery unleashed by years of German brutality. Whether they had been victims, perpetrators or bystanders of barbarity, people had to face the challenge of rebuilding their lives and re-establishing what was left of their families and communities. Across Germany, particularly in the Russian Zone and Berlin, soldiers looted civilians' homes and women and girls had been humiliated by their mass rape. There were few resources amidst a climate of starvation, distrust and grief.[5] At the war's end, Jewish survivors had no papers and no passports, and, in effect, no nationality, no official name, no home and no country to return to. Those survivors who did manage to return to their previous homes to search for relatives, or attempted to regain their properties, were frequently treated with open hostility by their former neighbours. Local people now living in homes stolen from Jews feared that the original owners would demand that their property and belongings be returned. In effect, there were no easy solutions; complex new laws required stolen homes and property to be the subject of a protracted legal process; claims needed to be submitted, and tardy legal prevarication would take years to resolve, if resolution was even possible.

The problem of restoring real estate and houses to their rightful owners quickly became a legal and moral nightmare. In the British Zone, during the 1950s, some 68,000 declarations of confiscated property had already been lodged, along with an estimated 35,000 legal claims under investigation. Of these, only a minor fraction could be resolved, or disposed of. In West Berlin alone, there had been 28,850 claims filed, of which 13,800 had been forwarded to the restitution agencies; only 450 could ever be resolved.

During the Third Reich, there were a number of organisations that included corrupt officials, lawyers and real estate brokers actively specializing in the 'Aryanisation' of Jewish buildings and real estate. Unscrupulous art dealers and auction houses enthusiastically set about plundering valuable Jewish artworks, while Goering succeeded in grasping the bulk of Jewish commercial assets for himself and the national treasury. But many thousands of Germans also became complicit in the spoliation by taking advantage of the knock-down purchase prices of former Jewish businesses, homes and household items. When evicting Jews from their homes, part of the eviction process involved the immediate disposal of their property, furniture and household effects by impromptu auctions, usually supervised by police as the occasions frequently resulted in hysterical 'grabbing' by the public. Such sales and transfers of property title from Jews to Germans had even been 'approved' by the authorities, making any legal restoration virtually impossible, such as occurred with the Jewish properties across Berlin seized by Speer's departments. Holocaust historian Peter Hayes, in a discussion aptly titled 'Learning How to Steal: Germany 1933-1939', summarizes the massive robbery of Jewish property in the German Reich:

> First came the 1933-1937 period: By the end of 1937, 60 percent of the roughly 100,000 Jewish-owned businesses in Germany as of 1933 had been liquidated or 'Aryanized' [sic] (i.e., taken over by non-Jews), the total wealth of German Jews had fallen by 40-50 percent, one third of the German Jewish population had fled the country, and nearly all of the Jews remaining were working for themselves or each other or unemployed and dependent on the community's relief measures.[6]

In the case of compensation for damages to the person, there were even more difficulties as no one knew who could be held responsible for imprisonment, maiming from torture and death. The whole question of reparation of stolen property was to haunt Germany into the twenty-first century, but by then the situation was naturally smoothed by the passage of time; most claims had either failed or were officially ignored, the claimants having died of old age.

It must not be overlooked that the millions of displaced people across Europe included a million Germans. These were German farmers and farm workers who had been encouraged to settle in lands conquered by the Third Reich, the so-called *Lebensraum*, or living space. These German settlers had forcibly taken over homes, land, and possessions from local people, often after they had been sent to concentration camps. After the war, over a million of these German settlers were forcibly, and frequently violently, expelled and sent back to Germany. Other ethnic Germans, whose families had lived for generations in border regions like the Sudetenland, also fled or were violently expelled. Allied opinion was divided about these expulsions. The Russians deemed the refugees' plight, including indiscriminate rape and looting, to be a form of natural justice in revenge for Germany's crimes. The British and American reaction was more caring, but they knew violence against the *Lebensraum* settlers would escalate unless they were swiftly returned to Germany. In a short time, the German populations living in Czechoslovakia, Hungary, Poland, Romania, and Yugoslavia, were expelled and returned to Allied-occupied Germany. Now homeless and impoverished, these Germans became unwelcome refugees in their own country, to be placed in camps for displaced persons and cared for by the Allied occupation powers.

For the surviving Jews, staying in Europe was always going to be difficult; their very existence was even dangerous. Historian Tony Judt wrote:

> After years of anti-Semitic propaganda, local populations everywhere were not only disposed to blame 'Jews' for their own suffering but were distinctly sorry to see the return of men and women whose jobs, possessions and apartments they had purloined. In the 4th arrondissement of Paris, on 19 April 1945, hundreds of people demonstrated in protest when a returning Jewish deportee tried to claim his (occupied) apartment. Before it was dispersed, the demonstration degenerated into a near-riot, the crowd screaming 'France for the French.'[7]

It was an untenable situation, which, as soon as was possible, encouraged many Jewish survivors to emigrate. When they were eventually able to obtain visas, most went to the United States, Latin America, South Africa, and to Jewish communities in Palestine.

On 14 May 1948, the British mandate on Palestine terminated. David Ben-Gurion, the chairman of the Jewish Agency for Palestine, announced the formation of the state of Israel. He declared:

> The Nazi Holocaust, which engulfed millions of Jews in Europe, proved anew the urgency of the re-establishment of the Jewish State, which would solve the problem of Jewish homelessness by opening the gates to all Jews and lifting the Jewish people to equality in the family of nations.

The announcement of the state of Israel opened the door for Holocaust survivors from Jewish refugee camps in Europe and Cyprus to enter the country. But that is another story. Unlike the millions of displaced persons living in abject poverty and misery in Germany and across Europe, for Speer, his post-war life was, in many respects, made bearable for him by being a prisoner of the Allies. Since 1933, Speer had moved comfortably among the very top Nazi ministers who could influence Hitler and Germany's war effort and economy. During 1939, Hitler's generals spearheading the invasion of Eastern Europe were financially rewarded for their successes, with Speer an integral part in facilitating the process.[8] It was therefore complicated for Speer to rehabilitate himself as the 'good German', knowing what he was hiding, and being aware that certain secrets might eventually come into the public domain. Speer lied about almost every aspect of his role in the Third Reich, including his acceptance and participation in its worst excesses. For several years, Speer's empire employed millions of slave labourers, many thousands of whom were deliberately worked to death. In 1941, Speer's department worked alongside the SS to build a motorway from Berlin to the Crimea, using Jewish slave labour and prisoners of war. Speer had also successfully hidden his involvement with building crematoria at Auschwitz; this only came to light when, in April 2015, an SS document dated May 1943, titled 'Professor Speer's Special Programme', was discovered by Berlin historian, Susanne Willems. The document proved Speer was one of the key individuals who made genocide possible, and that he knew what lay in store for the Jews being sent to Auschwitz. The report included Speer's handwritten advice which detailed the expansion of the mass extermination camp to 'become the solution to the Jewish question', a euphemism for extermination. It included the building of the infamous railway siding and ramp, where, on arrival at Auschwitz, victims were graded for slave labour or instant death. Auschwitz was not an isolated case; Speer also appointed two of his senior advisers, Desch and Sander, to investigate a number of other concentration camps around Germany and Poland. Had this secret SS report been seen by the Nuremberg judges, Speer would certainly have joined his partners in crime on the gallows.

Originally, at the time of being sentenced, Speer had appeared to have accepted his punishment, but following his release he began to suggest he had been too severely punished for crimes committed by others. When before the press and media, he appeared to have succumbed to a blanket of amnesia, and conveniently came to believe his own excuses, which warped his memory, rather than remembering his actual actions and participation in war crimes during his years of supporting Adolf Hitler. After his release from Spandau, and possibly disturbed by his conscience and confusion, Speer searched for redemption and he continued to do so until the end of his life, but he remained a troubled man. To ease his burden of guilt, he regularly sought absolution at the Maria Laach Benedictine Monastery on the south western shore of the Laacher See, near Andernach.

Speer began to believe his fellow countrymen actually wanted to forgive and even accept him back as a national figure. Journalists, academics and clergymen clambered to meet him and collectively united behind him helping to build his new image. To the German people, he became accepted as the clever wartime architect, the organisational genius who was innocent of the Holocaust, but bravely admitted his guilt on behalf of the German people, earning Speer a reputation that was convenient for millions of his countrymen. Germans could not believe that such a cultured, elegant and handsome professor was a war criminal, but, by him alone accepting responsibility, it gave them the means to forget what they too had known or done. Indeed it was necessary for Germans to believe someone important had stood up to Hitler, and in so doing, Speer's assurances could give them some hope of returning to a form of collective moral normality. Germans would need time for the healing process to take effect, and Speer would play an important part in his country's atonement. Such was German enthusiasm to hear and see Speer that he soon became a popular and well-known celebrity. However, the 2005 documentary film *Speer und Er* (Speer and Him) elicited an interesting observation from the film's director, Heinrich Breloer, who said Speer created a market for people wishing to deny harrowing knowledge by commenting 'believe me, I didn't know anything about it. Just look at the Führer's friend, he didn't know about it either.'

In 1970, Speer agreed to the publication of an illuminating piece of text in his biographical book *Inside the Third Reich*. One can only wonder how his Nuremberg trial might have ended had this admission been known to the Allied prosecutors. It reads:

> I had participated in a war which as we of the intimate circle should never have doubted, was aimed at world domination. What is more, by my abilities and energies I had prolonged that war by many months. I had assented to having the globe of the world crown that domed hall which was to be the symbol of the new Berlin. Nor was it only symbolically that Hitler dreamed of possessing the globe. It was part of his dream to subjugate the other nations. France, I had heard him say, many times, was to be reduced to the status of a small nation. Belgium, Holland, even Burgundy, were to be incorporated into his Reich. The national life of the Poles and the Soviet Russians was to be extinguished; they were to be made into helot peoples (slaves of ancient Greece). Nor, for one who wanted to listen, had Hitler ever concealed his intention to exterminate the Jewish people. Although I never actually agreed with Hitler on these questions, I had nevertheless designed the buildings and produced the weapons which served his ends.

Speer quickly settled down to enjoy his retirement and concentrate on writing well-paid accounts of his life, from the time he first met Hitler in 1930, until his release from Spandau Prison in 1966. He enjoyed giving lucrative interviews to an ever enthusiastic world media, portraying himself as the 'good German'. Through his autobiographies and interviews, Speer had carefully constructed an image of himself as a man who deeply regretted having failed to discover the monstrous crimes of the Third Reich. He continued to deny explicit knowledge of, and responsibility for, the Holocaust, although, through Speer's department, the *Schutzstaffel* (SS) built two concentration camps in 1938 and used the camp inmates to quarry stone for its construction. Writing in *Speer: Hitler's Architect*, its author, Martin Kitchen, states unequivocally that Speer was not telling the truth. He described Speer's oft repeated line that he knew nothing of the 'dreadful things' as 'hollow', because, not only was he fully aware of the fate of the Jews, but he was actively participating in their persecution. Likewise, when at Speer's behest a brick factory was built near the Oranienburg concentration camp, one of his staff commented on the poor conditions there. According to Kitchen, Speer stated, 'The Yids got used to making bricks while in Egyptian captivity.'[9] Speer was also fully aware that his departments were involved in the construction of a number of new concentration camps, at Flossenburg, Gross Rosen, Gusen and Oranienburg.

Nevertheless, in the years following his release, this image of the pleasant, kindly academic who 'knew nothing', dominated his historiography and gave rise to the 'Speer Myth'. The first part of the myth holds that, after his appointment as Minister of Armaments, he revolutionised the German war machine. The second is that he was a straightforward apolitical technocrat. It would not be until the 1980s that the myths began to fall apart after the armaments miracle was correctly attributed to Nazi propaganda. Adam Tooze wrote in his book, *The Wages of Destruction*, that the idea behind the second myth that Speer was just an apolitical technocrat was 'absurd'.[10]

Meanwhile, as part of the media process to rehabilitate himself and his fellow Germans, Speer travelled to London, a city he once sought to destroy, for an interview with the BBC. It was October 1973, and to escape media attention at Heathrow Airport, he travelled under a false name, but was discovered at Heathrow when an official, familiar with the Nuremberg trials, recognised him. Speer was temporarily detained but, following a call to the Home Office, he was allowed by the Home Secretary to enter the country on a special 48-hour pass to give the interview.

Subsequently, his various interviews were always interesting, but invariably cautious, and in no way were they probing; radio and television interviewers always treated him gently, which gave him the opportunity to sanitise his war-time role without being asked any hard or awkward questions. It is also understandable that none of his interviewers ever touched on his relationship with Hitler's mistress, Eva Braun; it was not public knowledge that Speer and Eva knew each other, or that the pair had spent long periods alone together, and over several years, no interviewer ever saw the significance. In any event, even if an interviewer had suspicions, the matter was left alone; after all, Speer was now a respected dignitary. Yet Eva was his big secret. His written accounts hardly mentioned her, and he would have been reluctant for his infidelity with her to become public knowledge, thereby tainting his new image of being the 'German gentleman'. But with Eva dead and now just a memory, Speer was a free man and famous. Not satisfied with returning to his wife, Margarete, it was not long before he commenced another secret extra-marital relationship with a much younger married German woman living in London, the wife of a former army officer. Once again, Speer kept this new relationship a close secret from everyone, especially from his wife, but the circumstances of his death brought the whole affair into the public domain.

This relationship commenced in the late 1970s; Speer received a letter from this young German woman. It seems she found life in England rather difficult, mainly due to the continued interest in the Second World War by the English.[11] Certainly, at that time, the subject of the holocaust was rarely out of the press being a popular subject for television programmes and films. For young Germans, faced with the steady and embarrassing flow of gruesome press accounts, newsreels and television reporting of the holocaust, growing up as 'normal' Germans was difficult; there were always the 'why' and 'how' questions to answer. This lady had read Speer's *The Secret Diaries* and felt that his book epitomised her belief that, somewhere, there must be a good German from that dark period. Speer was her man, so she wrote thanking him for his openness, and Speer replied, inviting her to visit him at his home in Mannheim. She accepted his invitation and thereafter they saw each other on a regular basis, the relationship soon resulted in clandestine trysts and secret holidays together, usually in the south of France. By all accounts, she was an attractive lady, slim and always well dressed, a suitable person for the self-assured and handsome Speer.[12]

At an indelicate moment in 1981, fate intervened. On Tuesday 1 September, Speer had been staying, under a false name, at the London Park Court Hotel, having been brought to London for another interview with the BBC. Following the interview, which took place with Speer in high spirits, he opted out of a BBC lunch as he already had an 'appointment'. Those who interviewed him that morning remembered him being very alert, friendly and enjoying himself. He then met up with his lady friend for lunch before they returned to his hotel. What then ensued is open to conjecture, but it was sufficient for him to collapse on their bed. The hotel security manager, a former police officer trained in first aid, was among the first to attend and tried to resuscitate him pending the arrival of an ambulance. Speer was rushed to St Mary's Hospital, accompanied by his lady friend, and it was only then that his identity was revealed, but it was too late. At the age of 76 years, Albert Speer died of a cerebral haemorrhage. His lady friend, who was conveniently staying near Speer's hotel, telephoned Frau Speer with the news of her husband's death. Frau Speer later commented that she had long since guessed there was someone else very close to her husband.

It came as no surprise to me to hear that Speer had died in a London hotel while enjoying the afternoon with his young lady. Even at 76, he was naturally attractive to all the ladies he came into contact with; he would openly flirt with lady journalists and interviewers, a character trait which had probably developed from his earlier relationship with Eva Braun.

Apart from his clandestine affairs, he also secretly acquired a number of stolen paintings during the war, which he managed to hide from investigators during his trial. Following his release from Spandau, these paintings were recovered and discreetly sold off to avoid any enquiries. As Speer kept his art deals a secret from his wife, it is probable the proceeds from the paintings paid for his secret assignations. After the war, such stolen paintings were known as 'rape art', and even where the original owners could be identified, most of these works of art were never restored to their rightful owners, or their heirs, due to the owners having been victims of the Nazis, or because of an unholy alliance of inadequate laws.[13]

But having got to know Speer reasonably well, I could begin to understand him, if not completely believe him. Hitler had mesmerised him, and Speer enjoyed the fame and fortune. Rather poignantly, and mainly due to Allied bombing, nothing remains of his personal architectural work, apart from an anonymous stretch of street lighting in Berlin. Perhaps he was correct when he later claimed it was his efforts as Hitler's armaments minister that saved most of Europe from the Russians. Speer's logic was that by his prolonging the war for three months, and maintaining munitions supplies to the German army fighting in the East, he could claim he enabled the Western Allies to advance sufficiently into Europe, while retarding the progress of Russia's army into Germany.[14] To his credit, towards the end of the war, if Speer can be believed, he did, unsuccessfully, try to find a way to kill Hitler, and when all was nearly lost for Germany he countermanded Hitler's orders for the destruction of German industry, knowing he and his family would be arrested and murdered as a consequence.

Under all the circumstances, a small part of me understands why he fudged the truth, and he certainly did not want to die on the gallows.

Later, on leaving the army, I was employed in West Germany as an interpreter. We lived in a small village on the outskirts of Hannover and soon made a host of local friends. When asked by Germans to explain my knowledge of their language, on suitable occasions I would comment that my teacher had been Albert Speer; unsurprisingly, few young Germans had even heard of Speer, who was then still a prisoner in Spandau.

As a civilian, I was reasonably free to enter and travel around communist East Germany, although such journeys by 'foreigners' were considered by the East German authorities as 'suspicious'. Each trip necessitated applying for a visa in advance, with one's route and hotel accommodation specified. Bumbling around East Germany was not possible. These trips were always interesting as every visiting foreigner was regarded as 'suspicious', and one was always under the watchful eye of the *Vopos*. Reporting daily to the local police station was mandatory; clearly my seemingly innocuous activities were presumed to be connected with my previous service in Berlin. For me, being followed by the *Vopos* was the norm.

In 1970 I returned to the UK to take up a full-time appointment with Kent Police. During my subsequent police career, I served for short periods with the Metropolitan Police, and in Sussex and Hampshire. There were a number of occasions when my German language skills were officially used, such as translating in court or interviewing German nationals. I once surprised and intrigued a course of senior German police commanders visiting the National Police College at Bramshill by giving them a lecture, in German, about policing the Channel Ports. When asked the anticipated question about my language ability, I explained my tutor was Albert Speer. Their level of astonishment was significant, and quickly gave way to curiosity, which resulted in having lunch with them and, then and there, receiving an invitation from their college director to join the German Police Staff College in Stuttgart for a three-month attachment. This offer clashed with a similar invitation from Cambridge University; but while pondering my options, fate intervened. I was on duty in the wrong place at the wrong time when I suffered serious injuries from an incident. Although a superintendent, I was unable to return to duty and, following multiple surgeries and long periods of hospitalisation, I settled in Kent with my family and began to write books; successfully, I'm pleased to say. I joined the lecture circuit and became a regular 'after dinner' speaker; my most requested talk was 'Guarding Rudolf Hess'. I still give the occasional talk to local school children who study the Second World War as part of the National Curriculum.

There is a final mystery. In March 1981, I received an unsigned postcard from London which reads, 'Albert Speer says Hello'. Oddly, the postcard depicted the Brandenburg Gate in Berlin. It was addressed to me at Canterbury Police Station when, at the time, I was the police Chief Inspector at Dover. That's life!

At this point in time my elderly aunt took me by surprise. Following the death of my mother in 1989, my aunt informed me I was part German. I learned from her that I had recent German ancestors; my maternal grandfather was Willy Emil Albers, known to the family as Grandpa Billy. Subsequent research revealed his family line originated in Kiel, northern Germany; his family then moved to Hamburg before settling in Nienburg near Hannover. All became clear when she told me that Willy, my grandfather, was a German child refugee whose family had been openly ostracized for their Catholicism (and possibly Jewishness) in Hamburg, then Luneburg, and had fled to England. Having been brought up in England, my grandfather spoke English without any hint of an accent; nevertheless, his background was clearly a family secret. My mother was therefore half-German, making me a quarter German.

On investigating my mother's family, I discovered that for a few months following the outbreak of the First World War, Grandpa Willy served as a ship's medical officer in the Royal Navy until his nationality was discovered. Towards the end of the war, he was permitted to work in France in an 'Aliens Battalion' as an Army medic.

Many years later, my research in Germany revealed that my grandfather was a direct cousin of Hans Albers, the most famous German actor and 'pop' idol between the two wars. Hans Albers served on the Western Front in the First World War and was very popular with Hitler until the Nazis discovered Hans's 'beau' was the very successful actress Hansi Burg of Jewish origin. The Nazis ordered the dissolution of their relationship, forcing Hansi to flee for her life, firstly to Switzerland and then to London. Hansi's father, the equally famous film director, Eugen Burg, was then arrested by the SS and, under the *Sippenhaft* law, executed in the Theresienstadt concentration camp. In 1946, Hansi returned to Germany and found Hans; they remained together until his death in 1960. The Wilhelmplatz, a square in Hamburg, Germany, is named after him.

On reflection: did I like Speer as an individual? Definitely.

Was he brilliant? Certainly.

A war criminal? Without doubt, yes.

Devious? Definitely. And clever at psychologically manipulating people.

My conclusion is that Speer, as a top Nazi, was too clever to be taken in by Hitler, and I believe he knew full well of everything that occurred in Nazi Germany, but turned a blind eye under the pretence of being 'too busy' to even consider the inconvenient truth. In part, he was living in a tightly delusional atmosphere shut off from the real world, but being intelligent he would have known this, and used it to assuage his conscience. He later admitted in his book *Inside the Third Reich* that 'any troublesome doubts were repressed…and, at a distance of decades I am staggered by our thoughtlessness in those years'. And I felt for him, he completely understood the significance of *Sippenhaft*; had he ever stepped out of line, been accused or arrested, his whole family and hundreds of associates would suffer the same fate. Nevertheless, following his release from prison in 1966, Speer always denied knowledge of a number of significant events that occurred during his long service as a Hitler minister, events then widely known across Germany; these included:

1. The national seizure of Jewish homes and property by his department, following the eviction of Jews from their homes to extermination camps in Poland. The acquisition of their buildings and homes in Berlin were within his gift to dispose of to his more important friends and colleagues. This was somehow overlooked at his trial.
2. The rise of the violent and anti-social SA and SS.
3. The Röhm *putsch* planning and executions of very senior state officials following the coup. He did later write that he had been vaguely aware of the operation.[15]
4. The brutal crushing of invaded countries and their populations.

5. His secret art collection.
6. The widespread locations across Germany of many hundreds of concentration camps, mostly staffed by local German civilians.
7. The half a million slaves that were working in his establishments by 1944. He claimed he helped them survive but some 40 per cent died of malnutrition, cruelty or neglect. He ambiguously wrote in his memoirs (*Erinnerungen*) 'the sight of people suffering affected my feelings but not my actions'.
8. The collapse of the concentration camp system originally designed and built by departments under his control, and the brutality and open mass murder that ensued. He later wrote:

> I was inescapably contaminated morally; from fear of discovering something which might have made me turn from my course, I had closed my eyes. This deliberate blindness outweighs whatever good I may have done or tried to do in the last period of the war. These activities shrink to nothing in the face of it. Because I failed at the time, I still feel, to this day, responsible for Auschwitz in a wholly personal sense.[16]

While the primary locations of concentration camps in Germany are well-known, their full extent is generally unknown. Speer's department would have had details of all camps and their sub camps, his department built them and many supplied essential labour for German industry, which he controlled. For example, Dachau had some 200 sub camps; Sachsenhausen 80; Buchenwald 130; Flossenburg 100; Neuengamme 120; Mittelbau-Dora 30; Mauthausen 65. Mauthausen was the only camp in Greater Germany with its own gas chambers. Bergen-Belsen had no known sub camps.

By late December 1944 the Allies were winning the war and advancing on Germany. SS leaders prepared orders to evacuate concentration camps in the east, including the extensive Auschwitz-Birkenau, and to relocate the camp prisoners nearer to or into Germany itself. The plan was to march them in massive columns without food or shelter in atrocious winter conditions. Accounts of these cruel and barbaric marches right at the very end of the war, with its probable million fatalities, have been overshadowed by the war's end. The proposed purpose of the marches was three-fold; firstly, there was an acute shortage of workers in Speer's factories, especially those involved in armaments, this shortage could be substituted by bringing in forced slave labour. Secondly, the SS leadership feared the approaching Russians would soon discover such camps and to reduce the effect of the voluminous evidence of mass murder and appalling brutality, orders were given to abandon camps and exterminate inmates too ill to be moved. Initially these orders were given to those camps in the immediate path of the advancing Russians, and then to camps about to be overrun by the Allies in the west. Such abandoned camps were to be destroyed to hide evidence of crimes against humanity. On receipt of the orders camp inmates were marched out into the winter snows in massive columns; it is estimated that between 10,000 and 15,000 from Auschwitz alone perished on the marches. Thirdly, the SS sought to retain control of the prisoners in case of camp uprisings; this was to be avoided as the SS anticipated such prisoners could be used to bargain with the Allies.

In Germany itself, camps were ordered to be evacuated and inmates marched cross-country to Bergen-Belsen, north of Hannover, for extermination. Some 700,000 prisoners were subjected to such marches across Germany, in winter and without food; it was later calculated that over a third died from malnutrition or the severe cold, or were murdered by their guards as they fell by the wayside.[17] Near Danzig, some 7,000 inmates, predominately women and children, were marched towards the coast where they were forced into the freezing sea under hails of machine gun fire.[18] Speer knew he could be called upon to share responsibility for, or knowledge of, such marches especially where inmates were forced to work in his failing industries. Accordingly, he subsequently recorded in his memoires that he (somewhere) made a speech, clearly to protect his back. He wrote of this speech in his *Inside the Third Reich*: 'The speech also called for surrendering prisoners, which included the Jews, unharmed, to the occupying troops, and stipulated that prisoners of war and foreign workers not be prevented from making their way back to their native lands.'

Even in the closing stages of the war Speer remained reluctant to comment on the depths the social landscape of German reaction had sank to. He continued to visit his industrial bases across Germany, many staffed by concentration camp prisoners, and witnessed at first hand the progressive degeneration in German society of ordinary people's lives and rights. It was a slow slide into the moral and physical brutalisation of a people who had initially and fanatically followed Hitler, only to end up in the apocalyptic horror as order broke down. German civilians, after all the miseries of war, were now exposed to the full extent of vengeful Nazi violence in addition to the limitless brutality and mass murder of camp inmates. Concentration camp death marches criss-crossed their shattered land, along with the mass shootings by the police and SS of exhausted prisoners who fell by the frozen wayside. Similar treatment was meted out to deserting German soldiers, mostly weary and shell-shocked, caught trying to return home and to young men found without military discharge papers, and indeed to anyone not openly enthusiastic about Nazi rule. Gestapo and police justice was instantaneous; it is estimated 15,000 soldiers died in such conditions; to put this into context, just 18 had been so executed in the First World War.[19] Conditions for German civilians were now unimaginable; millions of women were widows, 9 million German soldiers were prisoners and women headed most households.

For the ordinary German civilian there was nothing left except fear and dread, the stage was now set for the surviving, mostly homeless and starving population to assume the mantle of total victim. For them, not having previously concerned themselves with the fate and abuse of millions of Russians, Poles and Jews by predatory and bellicose Germans, the tables were now turned against them.[20] The few who could flee before the Russian advance did so but most civilians lacked transport and had no option but to await their inevitable fate.

It was during the years following Speer's death that his real involvement with concentration camps and support for the eradication of the Jews came to light. The same applied to his earlier ruthless seizure of Jewish homes and land for his *Germania*, the plan to rebuild Berlin. These seriously reduced the man in my estimation. I was, however, grateful to him for explaining his involvement with Eva Braun, and for admitting the reason behind his final visit to the Hitler bunker, an event not known or understood by previous historians and writers. His alleged influence on the American Air Force to use the atomic bomb against Japan has some logic.

Many of Speer's publicly recorded interviews can be listened to or watched on the internet. Sadly, for his descendants, nothing remains of his legacy as an architect, not even his majestic Reich Chancellery or the Zeppelinfeld stadium, which were both destroyed. His hard-earned reputation of being the 'good German' is now tarnished. Today his legacy as a Nazi war criminal holds firm.

I believe my experience interviewing Albert Speer in Spandau Prison was unique, especially having been a teenager at the time. Finally, during our lengthy conversations, Speer brought two items to my attention that gave me some cause for concern:

1. Goebbels' personal *Tagebuch* (diary) entry for 9 May 1941 reads:

> 'The Führer expresses his adamant certainty that, some day, the Reich will dominate all of Europe.'
>
> *Die Tagebucher von Joseph Goebbels.*
> Fröhlich, Elke. Munich 1998.

2. I once asked Speer the question, 'could it ever happen again?' Speer replied: 'read your history, the same factors will always give the same result'.

Today, in spite of the rise in German right-wing factions, modern Germans are willing to confront their horrific past, possibly because the perpetrators are long gone; holocaust museums and memorials abound and the subject is openly discussed in schools and in further education. On the occasion of the 75th Anniversary of VE day, German President Steinmeier said of VE day that, 'while the rest of the world was celebrating the end of the war, we made ourselves the enemy of the whole world.'

Appendix

Origin of the Swastika

*I, as leader, was unwilling to make public my own design, as it was possible
that someone else could come forward with a design just as good as, if not
better than my own. After innumerable trials I decided on a final form – a
flag of red material with a white disc bearing in its centre a black swastika.
And this is how it has remained ever since.*

Adolf Hitler

The swastika, or *Hakenkreuz* (from Sanskrit *svástika*), in its original
form was an ancient Indo-European religious symbol.

The Hitler family lived for several years in the town of Lambach,
Austria, located between Linz and Salzburg. The town was noted for its
Catholic Benedictine monastery and school, which Adolf attended, and
where Adolf sang in the boys' choir. Both buildings were decorated with
carved stones and woodwork portraying ancient religious swastikas.

The swastika was first seen on helmets of the Erhart Brigade, whose
motto was 'smashes all it meets' during the 1920 *putsch*. The brigade was
then taken over by the Nazis to become the SA.

Since the Second World War, the swastika has been exclusively associated
with the German dictator Adolf Hitler and the German atrocities of the
Second World War. Prior to the rise of Hitler, swastikas were an everyday
sight, used as the symbol of good luck and fortune. Across Europe and
the UK, swastika jewellery was popular, especially in the late 1930s.
Brands such as Coca-Cola and national sports teams often had the symbol
associated with them. The motif also formed the insignia of the US 45th
Infantry Division; their motif had to be abandoned in the run up to the
Second World War.

The international scout movement also used the swastika as the badge of
fellowship among Scouts world-wide, with its leader, Robert Baden-Powell,
proclaiming:

I want specially to remind Scouts to keep their eyes open and never fail to spot anyone wearing this badge. It is their duty then to go up to such a person, make the scout sign, and ask if they can be of service to the wearer.

Bibliography

Archived Documents
International Military Tribunal Report (Jewish Timeline, 1946)
The trial of German major war criminals: proceedings of the International Military Tribunal sitting at Nuremberg, Germany. Archived from the original on 17 August 2014.

Books
Beevor, Anthony, *Berlin: The Downfall 1945* (Penguin, 2003)
Bergen, Doris L., *War & Genocide: A Concise History of the Holocaust* (Rowman & Littlefield, 2003)
Bird, Eugene K., *The Loneliest Man in the World* (Secker & Warburg, 1974)
Blatman, Daniel *The Death Marches* (Harvard University Press, 2011)
Burleigh, Michael, *The Third Reich* (Macmillan, 2000)
Deschner, Karlheinz, *Das Jahrhundert der Barbarei* (1966)
Domarus, Max, *Hitler, Speeches and Proclamations: 1932–1945* (Bolchazy-Carducci, USA, 1962)
Fest, Joachim, *Die unbeantwortbaren Fragen: Notizen über Gespräche mit Albert Speer zwischen Ende 1966 und 1981* (Rowohlt Verlag, 2005)
Fest, Joachim, *Speer* (Wiedenfeld & Nicolson, 1973)
Flitner, Andreas, *Deutsches Geistesleben und Nationalsozialismus* (1965)
Förster, Jürgen, *Operation Barbarossa and the Final Solution* (2002)
Friedlander, Saul, *Nazi Germany and the Jews: The Years of Persecution 1933–1939* (Weidenfeld & Nicolson, 1997)
Fröhlich, Elke, *Die Tagebucher von Joseph Goebbels* (Munich, 1998)
Gellately, Robert, *Backing Hitler* (Oxford University Press, 2001)
Gerhard, Paul, *Schleswig-Holstein und das Hakenkreuz* (2001)
Goebbels, Joseph, *Joseph von Goebbels: Die Tagebücher, Teil 2* Fröhlich, Elke (ed.) (K.G. Saur Verlag, 1996)
Goldhagen, Daniel, *Hitler's Willing Executioners* (Abacus, 1997)
Greaves, Adrian, *The Bomb Whisperer* (Debinair Publishing, 2019)
Grunberger, Richard, *A Social History of the Third Reich* (Wiedenfeld & Nicolson, 1971)
Haswell, J., 'Eva Braun: The Lover Germany never knew Hitler had' (2017)
Hayes, Peter and Roth, John K. (eds.), *Learning How to Steal: Germany 1933–1939* (Oxford University Press, 2017)

Hayes, Peter, and Roth, John K., *The Oxford Handbook of Holocaust Studies* (2010)

Hitler, Adolf, *Mein Kampf* (1930)

Judt, Tony, *Postwar: A History of Europe Since 1945* (New York: Penguin Press, 2005)

Kellner, Friedrich, *Mein Widerstand* (My Opposition) (Wallstein Verlag, 2011)

Kershaw, Ian, *The Hitler Myth* (Oxford University Press, 1987)

Kitchen, Martin, *Speer: Hitler's Architect* (Yale University Press, 2015)

Lowe, Keith, *Savage Continent: Europe in the aftermath of World War II* (Penguin Books, 2012)

Macdonald, Callum, *The Assassination of Reinhard Heydrich* (Birlinn Ltd, 2007)

Neave, Airey, Major, *Nuremberg* (Hodder & Stoughton, 1978)

Nissen, Margret, *Sind Sie die Tochter Speer?* Dr Knapp, Margit, & Seifert, Sabine (eds.) (2005)

Schiefer, Jack, *Tagebuch eines Wehrunwürdigen* (Grenzland-Verlag, 1947)

Schlabrendorff, Fabian von, *The Secret War against Hitler* (Hodder & Stoughton, 1966)

Schmidt, Matthias, *Albert Speer: The End of a Myth* (St Martin's Press, 1984)

Schwendemann, Heinrich, *Strategie der Selbsvernictung* (Rusinek, 2004)

Sereny, Gitta, *Albert Speer: His Battle with Truth* (Macmillan, 1995)

Shirer, William, *The Rise and Fall of the Third Reich* (Secker & Warburg, 1960)

Speer, Albert, *Der Sklavenstaat Meine Auseinandersetzungen mit der SS* (Deutsche Verlags-Ullstein)

Speer, Albert, *Infiltration* (Ishi Press, 2010)

Speer, Albert, *Inside the Third Reich* (Orion Books, 1970, 1995 & 2003)

Speer, Albert, *Spandau: The Secret Diaries* (Collins, 1976)

Speer, Albert, *Spandauer Tagebücher* (1975)

Tarrant, V.E., *Jutland: The German Perspective* (Cassell Military, 1995)

Tooze, Adam, *The Wages of Destruction* (London, 2006)

Welch, Steven R., *German Military Justice in the Second World War: A Comparative Study of Court-Martialling of German and US Deserters* (Oxford Academic, 1999)

Willems, Susanne, *Der entsiedelte Jude: Albert Speer's Wohnungsmarktpolitik* (Berlin, Hentrich, 2000)

Periodicals

'The Trial of the Century – and of All Time', *Flagpole* magazine, 17 July 2002

Acknowledgements

I am grateful for the assistance and permissions willingly given by the staff at the following institutions:

The Jewish Museum (Berlin Holocaust Museum) Lindenstraße 9-14 Berlin.

Topography of Terror Museum and documentation Centre (site of the former SS and Gestapo Headquarters). Wilhelm- und Prinz-Albrecht Straße, Berlin.

Haus der Wannsee-Konferenz Museum. Wannsee, Berlin.

The German Resistance Memorial Centre and Museum, Stauffenbergstrasse, Berlin.

The Debling family for access to their extensive photographic collection and family papers dating from their residence in Spandau Berlin, pre-Second World War.

To my family and friends, who have finally succeeded in pushing me to publish this account as the 'last man standing' who, quietly over a period of two years, interviewed Albert Speer while he was still a war crimes prisoner in Spandau Prison.

I gratefully acknowledge the encouragement from Brigadier Henry Wilson at Pen and Sword when I was initially getting my thoughts together and for his thoughtful suggestions with the early drafts.

Testimonials to Date

Keith Lowe. Author and *Sunday Telegraph* **literary critic.**
A good solid account of the Second World War as witnessed by top Nazi, Albert Speer, Hitler's friend and right-hand man. For two years, as a young Army Officer, Adrian Greaves had unprecedented access to Albert Speer serving his twenty-year sentence in Berlin's Spandau Prison for war crimes. Greaves' account, based on his notes made at the time, make fascinating reading and remind us of the brutality and terror unleashed by Hitler's Nazi Germany. And as for Eva Braun, well!

Brigadier Mike Hill OBE
Historian and author, Adrian Greaves, seized on a remarkable opportunity to discuss with Albert Speer, then serving his sentence in Spandau Prison, Speer's true role with Hitler. Greaves' interviews and their publication uncover the truth behind this clever and distinguished war criminal and explain much about the incomprehensible and savage Third Reich.

Professor Richard Holmes. Historian and author.
As a young man Adrian Greaves was presented with the astonishing opportunity of regularly meeting with Hitler's top minister and friend, Albert Speer, in the infamous Spandau Prison. Not overawed by Speer, who befriended this young army officer, Greaves did not flinch from piercing the defensive and controversial mind of the senior surviving war criminal. Speer's revelations and opinions on a range of wartime events present much to reflect upon and Greaves' thoughtful conclusions reveal much about a terrible time for mankind.

(From Professor Holmes in 1991)

Brian Best. The Victoria Cross Society.
A stunning account from Adrian Greaves about Nazi Germany and its top Minister, Albert Speer, the so-called 'Good German'. After a series of interviews with Speer, Greaves came to understand this intriguing individual and uncovered many of his secrets. A riveting and stunning read.

Ian Knight. Author and broadcaster.
A revealing account recorded by Adrian Greaves when, still a teenager, he recorded his discussions with Albert Speer, a top Nazi war criminal in Berlin's notorious Spandau Prison. I'm pleased the persuasiveness of his friends finally encouraged the writing of his very revealing and frightening records.

Professor John Laband. Author and Historian.
As a young man Adrian Greaves was privileged to have access to a top Nazi war criminal in Spandau Prison following Europe's most terrifying decade. A story with a strong warning for the future.

About the Author

From 1961 Adrian Greaves enjoyed a three year short service commission with the Welch Regiment, mainly in West Berlin, where he met presidents Kennedy and Khrushchev and also witnessed numerous events along the Berlin Wall. While performing regular duties as guard commander at Spandau Prison, he was able to have regular and unique conversations with Albert Speer serving a twenty-year sentence for war crimes. Speer was once Hitler's friend and second-in-command for fifteen years. It is from these notes of their discussions, recorded at the time, that this book is based. After five years working in Germany as an interpreter, he joined Kent Police where he achieved high rank. He gained a BA in psychology before qualifying as a clinical psychologist and on retiring from the police service he was appointed the Kent Police psychologist. He has a Doctorate in South African and Zulu History. He has edited the *Journals of the Anglo-Zulu War Historical Society* since 1997 and has over twenty major books published, mainly relating to the Anglo Zulu War, and one major work on Lawrence of Arabia (*Mirage of a Desert War*).

He approaches his academic research with a detective's inquiring mind and by exploring the ground. He spent time in Berlin and Poland researching this work which has enabled new material to be included in this publication.

In 1964 the author met the ageing WWI poet and writer, Siegfried Sassoon CBE MC, who lived in a mansion near the Officers' Mess at Knook Camp at Heytesbury where Greaves was then stationed. Sassoon (8 September 1886–1 September 1967) was an English poet, writer, and soldier. Decorated for bravery on the Western Front, he became one of the leading poets of the First World War. On several occasions Greaves met socially with Sassoon and, on learning of his meetings with Albert Speer, Sassoon made him promise that he would, one day, publish his account. Here it is. Sassoon experienced a violent WWI.

Notes

Introduction
1. Assessment of Speer; British Prosecutor at the Nuremberg War Crimes Trials.
2. *Less than human: Why we demean, enslave, and exterminate others.* Livingstone Smith, David (St Martin's Press, 2011). Also, many Germans did not want their 'master race' to be diluted by the disabled and mentally handicapped who were viewed as a threat to Aryan genetic purity, and, ultimately, unworthy of life. By 1939, such individuals were collectively murdered under the Nazi directive known as 'T-4', meaning 'euthanasia'. T-4 was supervised and conducted by German doctors. After selection, victims were transferred to six medical institutions across Germany and Austria, where they were murdered in specially constructed gas chambers. Infants and small children were killed by injection or by starvation. The bodies of the victims were cremated. The T-4 program was deemed a 'success' and formed the blueprint for the later mass murder of Jews, Roma (Gypsies), and others. Despite public protests in 1941, the Nazi leadership continued this program until 1945. German T-4 records reveal a quarter of a million mentally and physically handicapped people were murdered between 1940 and 1945.
3. See Chapter 5.
4. *Nuremberg*, Neave, Airey, Major (Hodder & Stoughton, 1978).
5. *Speer: Hitler's Architect.* Assessment by historian Hugh Trevor-Roper, quoted by Kitchen. Kitchen, M. (Yale University Press, 2015).

Chapter 1
1. 1924 speech by Rector of Greifswald University; see *Deutsches Geistesleben und Nationalsozialismus*, Flitner, Andreas (1965).
2. *Jutland: The German Perspective* Tarrant, V.E. (Cassell Military, 1995).
3. Hitler's father, Alois Johann Schicklgruber, was born illegitimately in June 1837; his paternity was never established. He was a minor Austrian Customs official, and on being promoted, he applied to be legitimised in the name of his stepfather Hiedler, which was somehow entered in the official register of births as 'Hitler'. For reasons unknown, Alois always disliked his son Adolf.
4. *Nazi Germany and the Jews: The Years of Persecution 1933-1939* Friedlander, Saul (London, 1997).

5. *The Assassination of Reinhard Heydrich* Macdonald, Callum (Birlinn Ltd, 2007). While the ruthless Governor of Bohemia and Moravia, and head of Nazi security, Heydrich was assassinated in Prague by Czech military intelligence officers supported by the British Special Operations Executive. The successful operation, Anthropoid, unleashed a ferocious backlash against the local Czech intelligentsia.
6. Domarus, Max, *Hitler: Speeches and Proclamations 1932-1945.*
7. I did later tell Speer I had been inside the ruined Reichstag and asked him, as an architect, if the fire and the building's ruination affected him? 'No,' was his simple reply, which surprised me as I found the ruined building fascinating; the central staircase was still intact although riddled with bullet holes, and, with caution, one could get to the top with clear views across the city of East Berlin.
8. On 4 June 1942, Heydrich was assassinated in Prague by local resistance fighters trained by the British. For a full account, see *The Assassination of Reinhard Heydrich.*
9. It was first seen on the helmets of the Erhart Brigade during the 1920 *putsch.* Motto: 'Smashes all it meets'. The brigade was then taken over by the Nazis to become the SA.

Chapter 2
1. *Spandau: The Secret Diaries* Speer, Albert (Collins, 1976).
2. *Sind Sie die Tochter Speer?* Nissen, Margret, & Knapp, Dr Margit (Ed.) Sabine Seifert (2005).
3. *Inside the Third Reich* Speer, Albert.
4. *Speer: Hitler's Architect* Kitchen, Martin (Yale University Press, 2015). (See Appendix B for Jewish timeline).
5. *Die Tagebücher von Joseph Goebbels, Teil 2*, Elke, Fröhlich, (K.G. Saur Verlag, 1997).
6. *Tagebuch eines Wehrunwurdigen,* Schiefer, Jack, (Grenzland-Verlag, 1947).
7. *Speer* Joachim, Fest (Wiedenfeld & Nicolson, 1973).
8. *The Bomb Whisperer* Greaves, Adrian (Debinair Publishing, 2019). (Quoting Major Guy Lucas MBE, Corp of Royal Engineers).
9. At the war's end, Dr Gebhardt was arrested by the Allies and stood trial at Nuremberg in the special Doctors' trial, where he was convicted of war crimes and crimes against humanity. Speer had the final satisfaction of hearing that Gebhardt was sentenced to death; he went to the gallows in Landsberg Prison on 2 June 1948.
10. *The Rise and Fall of the Third Reich* Shirer, William (Secker & Warburg, 1960).
11. *A Social History of the Third Reich* Grunberger, Richard (Wiedenfeld & Nicolson, 1971).
12. *The Third Reich* Burleigh, Michael (Macmillan, 2000).
13. The Storch was a remarkably lightweight aircraft built for the specific task of being able to take off and land in just double its own length. In 1943 it

was put to the test when a force of German elite troops, led by Colonel Otto Skorzeny, crash landed by military gliders on the top of an Italian mountain where the deposed Italian leader Benito Mussolini was held prisoner by anti-German Italian troops, and rescued him. To get him off the 30-metre-wide mountain top, a Storch landed, and took on board both Mussolini and Skorzeny. Due to their corpulence, the plane had to commence its take-off down the mountain slope to treetop level at the valley below. Having gained enough speed, but having lost one wheel in the process, the plane became airborne and was flown back to base, safely delivering Mussolini.

14. *Albert Speer: His Battle with Truth*, Sereny, Gitta (Macmillan, 1995).
15. United States Strategic Bombing Survey reports. According to Speer, the increasing death rate of civilians from Allied bombing appeared to have little effect on the German population. Towards the end of the war, Speer remarked: 'the outlook of the people was often poor, but their behaviour was almost excellent'. See *The Strategic Air War against Germany, 1939-1945*, Forewords by Beetham, M., and Huston, J.W., Introduction by Cox, S. (London, 1998). For the population surrounded by secret police and informers watching for any dissenters, this official view is understandable. The American view was more realistic, opining that a third of Germans feared bombing the most. See *The Hitler Myth*, Kershaw, Ian (Oxford University Press, 1987).

Chapter 3

1. *Der entsiedelte Jude: Albert Speer's Wohnungsmarktpolitik* Willems, S. (Berlin, Hentrich, 2000).
2. *Speer: Hitler's Architect* Kitchen, Martin (Yale University Press, 2015).
3. In August 1946, Speer wrote to his wife, alluding to the threat of *Sippenhaft* (guilt by association):

> Most of the defendants have taken a very sour view of my activities during the last phase of the war. I can imagine pretty well what steps they would have taken had they found out at the time. There would not have been much left of the family.

4. *Das Jahrhundert der Barbarei* Deschner, Karlheinz (1966).
5. *Albert Speer: The End of a Myth* Schmidt, Matthias (St Martin's Press, 1984).
6. *Albert Speer: The End of a Myth* Schmidt, Matthias (St Martin's Press, 1984).
7. *Albert Speer: The End of a Myth* Schmidt, Matthias (St Martin's Press, 1984).
8. *Backing Hitler* Gellately, Robert (Oxford University Press, 2001).
9. *Speer: Hitler's Architect* Kitchen, Martin (Yale University Press, 2015).
10. *Schleswig-Holstein und das Hakenkreuz* Paul, Gerhard (2001).
11. *Speer: Hitler's Architect* Kitchen, Martin (Yale University Press, 2015).
12. Letters sold on 27 March at Bonhams for £18,000.

Chapter 5

1. *Speer: Hitler's Architect*, Kitchen, Martin (Yale University Press, 2015).
2. *Albert Speer: His Battle with Truth*, Sereny, Gitta (Macmillan, 1995).
3. *International Military Tribunal Report*.
4. 'The Trial of the Century – and of All Time', (part two). *Flagpole* magazine, 17 July 2002.
5. In 1944, Schacht, then the highly regarded finance minister largely responsible for the German financial recovery, was arrested by the Gestapo. His name appeared on the Stauffenberg conspirators' list but he was able to talk his way out of trouble, and was released. At the end of the war he was arrested by the Allies and charged with war crimes; he was found 'not guilty' and discharged.
6. 'The Trial of the Century – and of All Time', *Flagpole* magazine, 17 July 2002.
7. *Spandau: The Secret Diaries*, Speer, Albert (Collins, 1976).

Chapter 6

1. The Bendlerblock, the Army HQ where Count Claus von Stauffenberg was executed, now houses the National Museum of Resistance, and the street on which it stands has been renamed after him. His wife, Countess Nina von Stauffenberg was survived by her five children; her eldest son, Berthold, rose to the rank of General in the German Army.

    By the time of Colonel Count von Stauffenberg's attempted coup, he was already a national war hero, having been severely injured in North Africa. He was blind in one eye and had lost an arm, but was nevertheless appointed Chief of Staff to the Home Army. Following his failed coup to kill Hitler with a bomb, he was in Berlin awaiting news of the coup when he learned of its failure. On the news reaching Army HQ, Stauffenberg was immediately arrested, taken to the courtyard and shot. The attempted coup, known as Operation Valkyrie, is the subject of numerous books and films.

Chapter 7

1. John Profumo, UK Minister for War. Address to the Mons Officer Cadet Training Course, 1961 Commissioning Parade.
2. Checkpoint Charlie Museum data.
3. For the full account of our initial meeting, see Chapter 9, Spandau Questions.
4. The Third Reich: The first was in the Middle Ages, the second began in 1871 under Bismarck and Kaiser Wilhelm, the third was created by Adolf Hitler – his 'thousand year Reich', which lasted but twelve years.
5. The *Schutzstaffel* or SS, initially created as Hitler's personal bodyguards. The *Sturmabteilung* or SA. The Nazi Party's paramilitary organisation (or Brownshirts). (See following chapter for details).

6. Such as his biographer, Gitta Sereny.
7. *Speer: Hitler's Architect*, Kitchen, Martin (Yale University Press 2015).
8. 'Eva Braun: The Lover Germany never knew Hitler had', Haswell, J. (2017).

Chapter 9

1. *Mein Kampf* was disregarded at the Nuremberg war crime trials. It had been written prior to the war and its consideration was, therefore, beyond the remit of the court.
2. The Allied pre-trial holding camp at Kransberg Castle, used as a holding camp before the top Nazis were transferred for trial to Nuremberg. The castle was once renovated by Speer.
3. *Savage Continent: Europe in the Aftermath of World War II*, Lowe, Keith (Penguin Books, 1912). Following the fall of Berlin and for two weeks, the mass rape of German girls and women by Russian soldiers was deliberately encouraged by the Russian military. Rape was seen as a reward by the soldiers for their efforts, and punishment for the women for being German. Several thousand women committed suicide as a consequence. Across the Russian-occupied part of East Germany, post-war figures suggest some 2 million women and girls were raped in the immediate aftermath of the war. 1 out of 1.4 million women in Berlin were subjected to two weeks of mass rape with an estimated 200,000 'rape babies' later born to these unfortunate women; many of these babies were given up for adoption. For further details and statistics, see *Berlin The Downfall: 1945*, by Antony Beevor.
4. True, but with 650 years between the two events. In 1289, King Edward I was deeply in debt, and imposed an exorbitant tax on all Jews. Known as 'The Statute of the Jewry', the crown seized Jewish property and pressured the Jews to emigrate – but moving to Europe cost money and time. In London, some 680 Jews were imprisoned in the Tower, and 269 were executed for non-payment of dues. More executions of prominent Jews took place outside the capital. At the very same time, many remaining Jews were arrested in house-to-house searches across England and had their property destroyed or confiscated. Many more succumbed to state-promoted anti-Jewish plundering and murdering mobs. Jews caught escaping on the roads to the coast were frequently murdered as they sought refuge en route to the Channel ports. On 18 July 1290, the 'Royal Edict of Expulsion' expelled all remaining Jews from England; less than 2,000 remained, mostly women, children and the elderly. By November, virtually the whole community had left after two-and-a-quarter centuries. The edict was widely popular and met with little resistance, and the expulsion was quickly carried out. Most of the banished Jews had already fled to France, while others left for Spain, Germany and Flanders. Ships' captains were known to offload fleeing Jewish families on to sandbanks in the Thames Estuary and English Channel. They drowned and the crews absconded with the Jews'

possessions. The descendants of the surviving Jews did not return for 200 years.

5. Perhaps Frau Speer knew, or sensed, there was a relationship between the two. She would shortly discover even more about her husband's penchant for other ladies. In 1995, Speer's daughter, Hilde Schramm, unexpectedly inherited three paintings from her father's estate. They were art works her father had secretly acquired during the war at a time when he had access to stolen or seized Jewish property. At first, Schramm did not want anything to do with the paintings, since they lacked any provenance and almost certainly once belonged to Jews who were forced to sell or sign them away in order to survive. However, she decided to sell the paintings at auction and used the money, some £60,000, to fund a new charitable foundation, named Zurückgeben (to give back). Its commendable purpose was to raise funds for the support of Jewish women active in the world of science or the arts.

6. The American officials were George Ball, John Galbraith and Paul Nitze, US Bombing Survey.

7. *Speer: Hitler's Architect.* Neither his biographer, Fest, nor his publisher, Siedler, was able to get a satisfactory answer from Speer to this question. See *Die unbeantwortbaren Fragen: Notizen über Gespräche mit Albert Speer zwischen Ende 1966 und 1981*, Fest, Joachim (Hamburg, 2006).

8. 'Eva Braun: The Lover Germany never knew Hitler had', Haswell, J. (2017).

Chapter 10

1. *Killing Hitler: The Plots, the Assassins, and the Dictator Who Cheated Death*, Moorhouse, Roger (New York: Bantam Books, 2006).

2. *Valkyrie* Jones, Nigel (Pen & Sword, 2008).

3. a. *Operation Barbarossa and the Final Solution*, Förster Jürgen (2002).
   b. General Order from Field Marshal Walter von Reichenau, a distinguished and aristocratic Field Marshal reads:

   In the eastern theatre...the soldier must learn fully to appreciate the necessity for the severe but just retribution that must be metered out to the sub human species of Jewry... This is the only way we can remain true to the historic mission to free the German people once and for all from the Jewish/Asiatic menace.

   Field Marshal Walter von Reichenau.
   General Order to the 6th Army. 10 October 1941.

4. *Strategie der Selbsvernictung*, Schwendemann, Heinrich (Rusinek, 2004).

5. *War & Genocide: A Concise History of the Holocaust*, Bergen, Doris L. (Rowman & Littlefield, 2003).

6. *The Oxford Handbook of Holocaust Studies* (Peter Hayes and John K. Roth, eds., 2010).
7. *Postwar: A History of Europe Since 1945*, Judt, Tony (New York: Penguin Press, 2005).
8. Estates were gifted to senior officers, with farms being presented to noteworthy NCOs. In the case of Field Marshal von Kluge, he was personally rewarded by Hitler with a government cheque for 250,000 Reichmarks, with Hitler's own comment added to the cheque that 'half was to be spent on your estate and that Speer has received the necessary instructions'. See *The Secret War against Hitler*, Schlabrendorff, Fabian von (Hodder and Stoughton, 1966).
9. *Speer: Hitler's Architect*, Kitchen, Martin (Yale University Press, 2015).
10. *The Wages of Destruction*, Tooze, Adam (London, 2006).
11. I can sympathise with this sentiment. In 1970 I settled in England with a young German wife whose father, Fritz Klarhoefer, had been a Colonel in the German army. The Gestapo discovered he knew Count von Stauffenberg; it is unknown whether he had somehow been implicated in the failed assassination attempt on Hitler. He was, nevertheless, tracked down to his unit in Luxembourg and, during the final days of the war, assassinated under the *Sippenhaft* rule. His widow, my mother-in-law, somehow avoided arrest and post-war struggled to bring up her three small children, which she did with stoicism and much determination. In England, even by the 1970s, my wife was not always accepted or even made welcome socially, because of her German nationality and its association with the Nazis. As a qualified teacher, she nevertheless struggled for a couple of years with overt discrimination from within the profession and by some parents. She then, understandably, decided to return to Germany to take up a well-paid teaching position to match her qualifications
12. *Albert Speer: His Battle with Truth*, Sereny, Gitta (Macmillan, 1995).
13. 'Nazi Gemaelderraub: Kunst und Kunstverbrecher', (Nazi Painting Robberies, Art and Art Criminals. *Der Spiegel*, September 2007.
14. In the years that followed, I came to believe Speer's argument to counter the allegations that he had unnecessarily prolonged the war thereby causing the deaths of many Allied combatants still fighting German units and German civilians from Allied bombing. See *Inside the Third Reich* Speer, Albert (Wiedenfeld & Nicolson, 1970).
15. When interviewed by Gitta Sereny for her book *Albert Speer: His Battle with Truth*, Speer was able to remember some detail of the *putsch* and, without implicating himself, commented: 'When it was actually happening, of course one could hardly avoid being aware… as the streets were full of soldiers and there was a crisis atmosphere. And as I saw Hitler every day I knew he was perturbed.'

But, following his release from Spandau, questions about Speer's truthfulness soon began to surface. In 1971, Harvard University's Erich

Goldhagen alleged that Speer had been aware of the extermination of Jews, based on evidence that Speer had attended a Nazi conference in 1943 at which Himmler had spoken openly about 'wiping the Jews from the face of the earth'. Speer admitted that he had attended the first part of the conference but claimed he had left before Himmler gave his infamous 'Final Solution' speech, so therefore knew nothing about it. From his recently discovered ten-year correspondence with Helene Jeanty, the widow of a Belgian resistance leader, one of his letters confirmed he had listened to Himmler's speech about exterminating the Jews. The letters were sold at Bonhams in March 2007. Had the judges at Nuremberg known this, the outcome of Speer's trial could have been very different. He wrote: 'There is no doubt, I was present as Himmler announced on 6 October 1943 that all Jews would be killed. Who would believe me that I suppressed this, that it would have been easier to have written all of this in my memoirs?'

16. *Inside the Third Reich*, Speer, Albert.
17. *Todesmarsch*, Zonik, Zygmunt, Blatman (1967).
18. *Backing Hitler*, Gellately, Robert. See also *The Death Marches*.
19. *German Military Justice in the Second World War: A Comparative Study of Court-Martialling of German and US Deserters*, Welch, Steven R. (1999).
20. *Interrogations: The Nazi Elite in Allied Hands, 1945* Overy, R.J. (London, 2001).

Index